• Shelley Melvin received her formal training with Simone Beck at l'Ecole des Trois Gourmandes, in France. She has worked as a caterer, cooking instructor and consumer advisor for a major food processor manufacturer. Her previous books are *Not Just Cheesecake! The Low-Fat, Low-Cholesterol, Low-Calorie Great Dessert Cookbook* and *Quick & Easy*.

• Marilyn Stone, a member of the International Assn. of Cooking Professionals, has worked as a cookbook editor in the publishing industry. She is the author/editor of *The Chosen: Appetizers and Desserts* and co-author of *Not Just Cheesecake!*

• Gail Kauwell is an assistant professor in the Clinical and Community Dietetics Program at the University of Florida. She was named the 1988 Distinguished Dietitian of Florida by the Florida Dietetic Association.

The recipes in *Snack to your Heart's Content!* give snack options beyond carrot sticks and air-popped popcorn. But remember, even nutritious foods must be eaten in moderation —overeating is never healthful.

Consult your physician if you are on a medically restricted diet.

SNACK

TO YOUR HEART'S CONTENT!

The Low-Fat, Low-Cholesterol, Low-Calorie
Quick & Easy Cookbook

By Shelley Melvin and Marilyn Stone

Foreword by Gail Kauwell, M.Ag., R.D.

TRIAD PUBLISHING COMPANY
GAINESVILLE, FLORIDA

Printed in the United States of America

Library of Congress Cataloging-in-Publication Data
Melvin, Shelley, 1944-
Snack to your heart's content! : the low-fat, low-cholesterol, low
-calorie quick & easy cookbook / Shelley Melvin and Marilyn Stone;
foreword by Gail Kauwell.
p.   cm.
ISBN 0-937404-32-2
1. Low-fat diet--Recipes.   2. Low-cholesterol diet--Recipes.
3. Low-calorie diet--Recipes.   4. Cookery (Yogurt cheese)
5. Snack foods.   I. Stone, Marilyn.   II. Title.
RM237.7.S54   1990   89-20401
641.5'63--dc20
CIP

Illustrations: Lea Gabbay
Cover photo: John Moran

Published and distributed by Triad Publishing Co., Inc.
1110 Northwest 8th Avenue, Gainesville, Florida 32601.
For information on bulk orders write Special Sales Dept.

• CONTENTS

• FOREWORD

by Gail Kauwell, M.Ag., R.D.

Everyone loves to snack—kids, teens, adults and senior citizens alike. The problem is, so many snack foods are high in calories, fat and cholesterol and relatively low in vitamins and minerals. Consequently, snacking is often thought of as being bad for you.

However, eating lighter meals interspersed with nutritious snacks can be just as healthful as a "three meals a day routine," providing you make sensible choices. With the easy availability of yogurt cheese, nutritious and satisfying snacks don't have to be limited to carrot and celery sticks anymore. Yogurt cheese can be used to make a variety of new and different foods, like pocket lasagna and ice cream softies, as well as low-calorie, low-fat versions of such familiar snacktime favorites as pizza or banana bread.

Health conscious people interested in modifying their eating habits to reduce their risk of developing chronic problems like heart disease and obesity will find the snacks in this book a great way to satisfy the munchies without wreaking havoc with their diets. Parents interested in helping their children develop healthy eating habits will also love having these ideas available for lunch box treats, after-school nibbles, picnics, parties or any occasion that calls for a snack.

So next time you want a snack that's quick to make, fun to eat and tastes delicious, try one of these recipes and feel good about the healthy choice you've made.

• INTRODUCTION

I love food! I love its colors, textures, flavors, aromas and tastes. I have also had a weight problem since the age of 12.

Like many people, my problem is not usually at mealtime; I am an after-dinner snacker. But carrot sticks or an apple simply are not satisfying. I want potato chips, peanut butter, cookies, ice cream, cheese and crackers!

I had to learn to control these cravings.

I finally did, with the discovery of a versatile, "perfect" food called yogurt cheese, and a gadget called a Yogurt Cheese Funnel that makes yogurt cheese by draining the liquid whey out of yogurt. I haven't looked back.

First, I blended it with a packaged onion soup mix, and couldn't tell it wasn't made with sour cream! So, with my spice cabinet open and garlic press handy, I started mixing and matching until I had a nice little repertoire of low-fat dips and spreads that tasted rich and creamy.

With many new tastes to choose from, it was a small step from dip to salad dressing. I added the new mixtures to tuna and then to chicken, fish and potatoes. (What's interesting is that the salad combinations can usually be turned back into spreads or dips.) It's also great to be able to have a tossed salad with thick creamy dressing.

Next I added yogurt cheese to baked goods and reduced the fat. Many of these experiments worked, and the results were

9

exciting! Now I can count on a collection of cakes and breads that don't spoil my diet.

Yogurt cheese is so easy to work with that you, too, can do what I've done here. You can "de-fat" and "decalorize" your own favorite recipes by substituting yogurt cheese for cream cheese, sour cream and mayonnaise. For those times when you crave something that's "forbidden," you may be able to have just a little by combining it with yogurt cheese to make it low*ER* in fat and calories. The cheese takes on the flavor of whatever it's mixed with.

People diet for different reasons and in different ways. I am a Weight Watcher and I use my milk exchanges for snacking. In testing the recipes for this book, I kept in mind how they would fit into my program. What could be better than a cup of cream soup that counts as one milk and two vegetables? (The exchanges I used are available on request.) For those of you on other programs and diets, each recipe includes nutritional information and the exchanges developed by the American Diabetes Association and American Dietetic Association.

Just about everyone seems to be on a diet of some sort— to lose weight, lower cholesterol, or reduce sodium intake. Yet it is hard to stay on a diet that is bland, boring, tasteless or unsatisfying. Now when that hungry feeling attacks between meals, you have a selection of tasty snacks that fit into your total dietary plan.

I hope you'll enjoy these recipes as much as I do and that you can finally Snack to Your Heart's Content!

SHELLEY MELVIN
JANUARY, 1990

• BEFORE YOU BEGIN

All the recipes in *Snack to your Heart's Content!* are made with yogurt cheese, so let's begin at the beginning: how to make yogurt cheese the easy way.

I recommend that you include a Yogurt Cheese Funnel* as part of your basic kitchen equipment. With a Funnel, having yogurt cheese can be as easy as spooning yogurt from the carton. Not only is it effortless, the cheese unmolds cleanly, eliminating all the mess of old-fashioned methods. (But if you don't have a Funnel, cheesecloth or any fine-mesh strainer may be used.)

Yogurt Cheese Recipe

1 16-ounce carton plain non-fat yogurt (without gelatin)
1 Really Creamy® Yogurt Cheese Funnel™

Spoon yogurt into the Funnel (placed over a tall glass) and put in the refrigerator. Allow liquid whey to drain 2 to 24 hours, until cheese is the desired consistency.

Discard whey. Keep cheese refrigerated in a covered container. Whey may continue releasing, so pour off any accumulated liquid before using.

---

*The Really Creamy Yogurt Cheese Funnel is available in kitchenware shops and catalogues and health food stores.

How to tell when the cheese is "done"

The total liquid that will drain from the yogurt is about half its quantity. With a 16-ounce carton, you will have 7 or 8 ounces of whey. In most cases this will take 8 to 12 hours. If you want the cheese to be as firm as possible, let it drain up to 24 hours.

The brand of yogurt also has an effect (there is a wide, normal variation in how yogurt drains). For example, in 2 hours the amount of whey (from 16 ounces of yogurt) can range from 2.5 ounces to 6 ounces; once you start working with your favorite brand, you will learn how to plan.

Which yogurt to use

You can use any natural yogurt, either plain (non-fat or low-fat) or flavored (vanilla, lemon, coffee) that does not contain gelatin. Gelatin holds the whey in the yogurt and does not allow it to drain off.

Sometimes you will find a carton of yogurt without gelatin that does not release its whey. This may be due to the processing temperature. Try a carton from another batch or a different processing plant (that information is on the label), or use another brand of yogurt for a while.

Mixing, cooking and freezing

Yogurt cheese has a creamy, spreadable consistency that mixes easily. (You can mix it with anything from a wire whisk to a food processor or blender.)

Like all milk products, yogurt cheese is sensitive to heat. Heat very gently and do not allow to boil. You can prevent separation or thinning of the cheese during cooking by combining it with flour or cornstarch. Before mixing hot foods with yogurt cheese, cool them slightly. Another option is to stir a little of the hot food into the cheese to warm it, then slowly add the cheese to the hot food, stirring constantly. It is best to add yogurt cheese to hot foods at the end of the cooking time.

Yogurt cheese freezes well; if the texture becomes grainy, stir until smooth.

More nice things about yogurt cheese

As you become acquainted with yogurt cheese, you'll soon discover its wonderful versatility. It's the perfect substitute for cream cheese and other soft cheeses, sour cream, and even mayonnaise because it's much lower in fat and calories, and has the quality of taking on any flavor it's mixed with. Its own flavor is part way between cream cheese and sour cream, varying with milkfat content and brand of yogurt.

As a rule, quantities are not critical. By tasting as you mix yogurt cheese with other ingredients, you can easily change any recipe or create your own.

The flexibility of yogurt cheese allows some recipes to have multiple uses: a spread can be a potato topping; a dip can become a soup. Yogurt cheese mixtures are never boring because they can be used in many ways and for many different types of snacks.

More about the Yogurt Cheese Funnel

The Really Creamy Yogurt Cheese Funnel has a special microsized mesh lining that creates an exclusive wicking system for fast whey removal. It is constructed from pure plastic polymers, making it durable and easy to clean. When firm, the cheese unmolds cleanly. Many diet and nutrition authorities use and recommend the Funnel.

"When a recipe calls for low-fat, high-calcium yogurt cheese, you'll be glad to have a . . . Funnel on hand."
(Weight Watchers magazine)

"The perfect gift for the low-cholesterol cook."
(Florida Times-Union, Healthy Heart column)

"Making fresh, tangy yogurt cheese is easy thanks to the . . . Funnel."
(Food & Wine)

• HOW TO USE THE BOOK

Organization
In each chapter, the recipes are arranged roughly according to number of calories, from lowest to highest.

Serving size
How big is a snack? That depends on so many factors that most of the recipes do not suggest a serving size (or number of servings). The quantities used for the nutritional analyses are not intended to be recommended portions.

Nutritional analysis
Whenever more than one choice is given for an ingredient or an amount, the nutritional information for the recipe is based on the first one listed. Any ingredient called "optional" has *not* been included in the analysis.

All nutrient analyses are approximate; actual values may vary depending on season, brand of product used, etc. Nutritional values of yogurt cheese will also vary with draining time and method used.

Exchanges are based on the 1986 revision of *Exchange Lists for Meal Planning* developed by the American Diabetes Association and the American Dietetic Association.

More nutritional information

• *Comprehensive list.* A table (page 177) lists nutritional information for most recipe ingredients as well as for optional ingredients and accompaniments. A few non-recommended options are also included for making comparisons.

• *Cheese.* Some recipes include Cheddar and other cheeses that, as everyone knows, are high in fat and cholesterol. By combining these high-fat cheeses with yogurt cheese and other ingredients, the fat and cholesterol are lowered so you may be able to allow yourself a small amount without breaking your diet. In many recipes, reduced-fat cheeses may be substituted.

• *Eggs.* When eggs are called for, most recipes use egg whites (lower in fat and cholesterol) instead of whole eggs. (A cholesterol-free product such as Egg Beaters may be substituted. Refer to the package for instructions and nutrition information.) If your diet allows it, one whole egg may be substituted for two egg whites in many recipes.

• *Sodium.* Although the book is not specifically designed for low-sodium diets, most of the recipes are low in sodium or offer options for reducing sodium. More and more manufacturers are producing reduced-sodium foods, so read the labels and you will find it easier than ever to cut down. Herb seasoning mixes are a great substitute for the salt shaker.

• *Sweeteners.* In recipes for sweet snacks, the sweetener has been used sparingly in order to reduce calories without sacrificing taste. In most cases, another sweetener can be substituted, such as honey, maple syrup, grain sweetener, fruit juice concentrate, fruit spread, or all-fruit jams (conserves) sweetened with fruit juice (no added sugar). If you use an artificial sweetener for baking, make sure the product you are using can be heated. The choice is up to you, based on your individual dietary needs.

1 • DIPS AND SPREADS

A remarkable feature of yogurt cheese is its versatility. In this chapter, for example, most of the dips and spreads can be interchangeable according to how much liquid is added. And just about any of them can be used in other ways, such as soup . . . or potato topping . . . or pasta salad dressing. It's easy to experiment. So use your imagination!

The recipes are arranged by calories from lowest to highest. The nutritional information in most cases is based on one-fourth cup (4 tablespoons) of the mixture, enough to cover eight crackers generously. The size of your snack, however, is up to you.

Whether you're snacking on party leftovers or creating your own nibble, a dip or spread doesn't stand alone. The food used for scooping it up or spreading it on will affect your intake of fat, cholesterol and calories, so be aware of the total snack (don't think it "doesn't count" if it's not in the analysis!).

Vegetables are a good low-fat, low-calorie accompaniment. Eat them raw or blanched in boiling water (or briefly steamed), refreshed in cold water, then chilled. Here are some ideas (their nutritional values are on the table beginning on page 177):

Artichoke hearts or leaves (cooked)
Asparagus spears
Bell pepper strips: red, green or yellow

17

Banana peppers, charred and peeled
Belgian endive spears
Broccoli and cauliflower flowerets
Brussels sprouts, small or cut in half (cooked)
Carrot sticks
Celery sticks
Cherry tomatoes
Cucumber rounds or hollowed out chunks
Green beans
Mushrooms and mushroom caps
Potatoes, tiny
Radishes
Snow peas
Sugar snap peas
Squash slices or spears (yellow or zucchini)
Turnip slices

Hard-cooked egg white halves can also be filled with a dip.

When buying crackers, read the labels for nutritional information. The lower fat and calorie choices include melba toast rounds, water crackers, saltines, rice cakes, Ry Krisp, Ryvita, and whole grain crackers such as Kavli. There are recipes in Chapter Seven for corn chips and pita chips that are baked without adding any fat.

For serving dips and spreads at a party, prepare an attractive vegetable container such as a scooped-out eggplant, red cabbage or bell pepper, or a hollowed-out loaf of round crusty bread. But don't be surprised when guests let you know that these recipes are "too rich" for their diet. It happens all the time!

Gazpacho Dip

This also makes a nice potato topping.

1   medium-size cucumber, peeled and seeded
1   cup non-fat yogurt cheese
1/4   teaspoon ground cumin
1/2   peeled, seeded and cubed tomato
1/4   cup minced green onion

Chop cucumber finely and drain well in a colander. Pat dry with a towel.

In a medium-size bowl, whisk the yogurt cheese and cumin until well blended. Gently stir in the cucumber, tomato and green onion. Cover and chill until serving time.

Makes about 1³/₄ cups.

Per 1/4 cup: Calories 29; protein 3 gm; carbohydrates 4 gm; fat <1 gm; cholesterol 0 mg; calcium 86 mg; sodium 25 mg. Exchanges: 1 vegetable.

Spinach Dip

A low-cal version of an old standby.

1 package (10 oz.) frozen chopped spinach, thawed
1½ cups non-fat yogurt cheese
1 tablespoon dried dill weed
¼ teaspoon Tabasco sauce
½ cup chopped green onions
½ cup chopped fresh parsley

Drain the spinach, then squeeze out as much liquid as possible. Chop finely.

In a medium-size bowl, whisk yogurt cheese with dill and Tabasco sauce until smooth. Add the spinach, green onions and parsley and mix well. Cover and chill until serving time.

Makes about 2½ cups.

Per 1/4 cup: Calories 35; protein 4 gm; carbohydrates 5 gm; fat <1 gm; cholesterol 0 mg; calcium 138 mg; sodium 51 mg. Exchanges: 1/2 skim milk.

Indian Carrots

*This is also a tasty condiment to accompany
highly seasoned meat dishes and curries.*

1 large carrot, peeled and trimmed
1 cup non-fat yogurt cheese
1 teaspoon light brown sugar
1/4 teaspoon ground cumin
    Dash Tabasco sauce, or more to taste
1/4 cup finely minced onion

Cut the carrot into short julienne strips (or grate coarsely).
There should be about 1 cup. Drop into boiling water and blanch
for 30 seconds. Drain and pat dry with a towel.

In a medium-size bowl, whisk yogurt cheese, sugar, cumin
and Tabasco until smooth and well blended. Stir in carrots and
minced onion. Cover and chill until serving time.

Serve with crackers or fresh vegetables. Can also be used
as a sandwich filling.

Makes about 1 1/2 cups.

Per 1/4 cup: Calories 40; protein 3 gm; carbohydrates 6 gm; fat <1 gm; cholesterol 0 mg; calcium 101 mg; sodium 34 mg. Exchanges: 1 vegetable.

Sage-Derby Cheese

A dieter's version of the famous English cheese.

1 cup non-fat yogurt cheese
2 tablespoons minced green onion
1 tablespoon dried sage
2 tablespoons poppy seeds, optional garnish

Combine all ingredients in a medium-size bowl and whisk until well blended. Cover and chill until serving time. If desired, sprinkle with poppy seeds just before serving.
Makes about 1 cup.

• **What makes yogurt cheese special is that it picks up the flavor of whatever it's mixed with.**

Per 1/4 cup: Calories 42; protein 5 gm; carbohydrates 5 gm; fat <1 gm; cholesterol 0 mg; calcium 151 mg; sodium 40 mg. Exchanges: 1/2 skim milk.

Middle Eastern Mint Dip

The exotic flavor goes especially well with cucumbers.

1 teaspoon cumin seeds
1½ cups non-fat yogurt cheese
 Salt, optional
2 tablespoons minced fresh mint leaves

    Toast the cumin seeds in a small dry skillet over moderate heat, shaking the skillet until the seeds turn darker and begin to pop. Pulverize the seeds with a mortar and pestle, blender or spice grinder.

    In a medium-size bowl, whisk yogurt cheese, cumin seeds and salt until well blended. Add the mint leaves and mix well. Cover and chill until serving time.

    Makes 1½ cups.

Per 1/4 cup: Calories 42; protein 5 gm; carbohydrates 4 gm; fat <1 gm; cholesterol 0 mg; calcium 145 mg; sodium 41 mg. Exchanges: 1/2 skim milk.

Vegetable Dip

You can create your own vegetable combinations from radishes, cucumbers, zucchini, red bell peppers or green onions.

1½ cups non-fat yogurt cheese
1 tablespoon finely grated carrot
2 teaspoons finely grated onion
1 teaspoon finely grated green bell pepper
1 small clove garlic, minced
Dash white pepper
Salt, optional

In a medium-size bowl, whisk yogurt cheese with carrot, onion, green pepper, garlic and seasonings until well mixed. Cover and chill until serving time.

Makes about 1½ cups.

Per 1/4 cup: Calories 42; protein 5 gm; carbohydrates 5 gm; fat tr; cholesterol 0 mg; calcium 141 mg; sodium 41 mg. Exchanges: 1/2 skim milk.

• *Variation (all amounts approx.).* With a food processor, chop 1/2 medium onion, 1 or 2 carrots, 1/2 green bell pepper, 2 stalks celery with leaves, 1/2 cucumber, 4 or 5 unpeeled radishes and 1 clove garlic. Transfer to a fine sieve and press with a spoon to remove liquid from vegetables. Blend with 1 1/2 cups yogurt cheese.

Quick Herb Cheese #1

1 cup non-fat yogurt cheese
1 small clove garlic, minced
2 tablespoons finely minced fresh parsley
1 teaspoon dried oregano
1/2 teaspoon lemon juice
1/8 teaspoon freshly ground black pepper
    Dash ground red pepper (cayenne), or to taste

Combine ingredients in a medium-size bowl and whisk until well blended. Cover and chill until serving time.
Makes 1 cup.

Per 1/4 cup: Calories 43; Protein 5 gm; Carbohydrates 5 gm; Fat <1 gm; Cholesterol 0 mg; Calcium 140 mg; Sodium 41 mg. Exchanges: 1/2 skim milk.

Quick Herb Cheese #2

Tastes like an expensive French brand (but without the fat!).

1 cup non-fat yogurt cheese
1 clove garlic, minced
1 teaspoon caraway seed
1 teaspoon dried basil
1 teaspoon dried dill weed
1 teaspoon snipped fresh chives

Combine all ingredients in a medium-size bowl and whisk until blended. Cover and chill until serving time.
Makes 1 cup.

Per 1/4 cup: Calories 45; protein 5 gm; carbohydrates 5 gm; fat <1 gm; cholesterol 0 mg; calcium 157 mg; sodium 81 mg. Exchanges: 1/2 skim milk.

• ***Quick Herb Dip #3.*** Blend your favorite herb seasoning into plain yogurt cheese and use for a dip, baked potato topping, or thin to taste for a salad dressing. Use about 1 to 2 tablespoons of seasoning per cup of yogurt cheese. Let your taste be your guide.

Budapest Spread

1 cup non-fat yogurt cheese
1 anchovy fillet, coarsely chopped, or more to taste
1 tablespoon finely chopped green onion
1 tablespoon chopped capers
$1/2$ teaspoon paprika
$1/2$ teaspoon anchovy paste*
    Pinch ground red pepper (cayenne)

    Place all ingredients in a medium-size bowl and whisk until smooth. Cover and chill several hours or overnight.
    Makes about 1 cup.

    Note: An additional anchovy may be substituted for the anchovy paste.

Per 1/4 cup: Calories 43; protein 5 gm; carbohydrates 5 gm; fat <1 gm; cholesterol 0 mg; calcium 144 mg; sodium 74 mg. Exchanges: 1/2 skim milk.

Dilly Dip #1

1 cup non-fat yogurt cheese
1 tablespoon minced onion
1 teaspoon dried dill weed
1 large clove garlic, minced

Combine all ingredients and whisk well. Cover and refrigerate several hours to blend flavors.
Makes 1 cup.

- *Variation:* Add 1 teaspoon minced fresh parsley or $3/4$ teaspoon beau monde seasoning (or both).

Per 1/4 cup: Calories 43; protein 5 gm; carbohydrates 5 gm; fat tr; cholesterol 0 mg; calcium 146 mg; sodium 41 mg. Exchanges: 1/2 skim milk.

Dilly Dip #2

³/₄ cup non-fat yogurt cheese
¹/₄ cup chopped fresh dill, or 1 tablespoon dried dill weed
     Tabasco sauce to taste
  8 pickled cocktail onions, coarsely chopped

In a medium-size bowl, whisk the yogurt cheese, dill and Tabasco until smooth. Blend in chopped onions. Cover and chill until serving time.

Makes about ³/₄ cup.

Per 1/4 cup: Calories 44; protein 5 gm; carbohydrates 5 gm; fat tr; cholesterol 0 mg; calcium 158 mg; sodium 165 mg. Exchanges: 1/2 skim milk.

Diet note: To lower sodium, substitute 1 tablespoon finely chopped green onion and a few drops vinegar for the cocktail onions.

Marvelous Dip

2 cups non-fat yogurt cheese
1 clove garlic, minced
1/2 cup finely chopped red onion, or less to taste
1 tablespoon chopped fresh parsley
1 tablespoon lemon juice
1 teaspoon dried Italian herbs
1/2 teaspoon white wine Worcestershire sauce
1/8 teaspoon curry powder

Combine all ingredients in a large bowl and whisk until well blended. Cover and chill until serving time.

Makes about 2 cups.

Per 1/4 cup: Calories 45; protein 5 gm; carbohydrates 5 gm; fat <1 gm; cholesterol 0 mg; calcium 147 mg; sodium 44 mg. Exchanges: 1/2 skim milk.

Thistle Dip

1 jar (6 oz.) marinated artichoke hearts, drained
$^1/_2$ small onion, coarsely chopped (about 2 Tbsp.)
1 cup yogurt cheese
   Dash ground red pepper (cayenne)

   Process the artichoke hearts in a food processor or blender until completely smooth. Transfer to a bowl and stir in remaining ingredients. Cover and chill at least 1 hour.
   Makes about 1$^1/_4$ cups.

Nutritional information is not available for marinated artichoke hearts.

- *Lo-Cal California Dip.* If you make this popular dip from onion soup mix and sour cream, use yogurt cheese instead of sour cream. It will taste the same, but fat and calories will be way, way down.

Caraway Cheese Spread

Try it with bell peppers — green, red, or yellow.

2 teaspoons caraway seeds
$^3/_4$ cup non-fat yogurt cheese
$^1/_2$ teaspoon very finely minced onion
$^1/_4$ teaspoon Dijon-style mustard
$^1/_8$ teaspoon salt, or to taste
   Freshly ground black pepper

Grind the caraway seeds finely using a mortar and pestle, blender or spice grinder.

Combine remaining ingredients in a small bowl and whisk until smooth. Blend in the caraway seeds. Cover and chill until serving time.

Makes about $^3/_4$ cup.

> • ***Quick Tip.*** Most dips and spreads can become "instant recipes" by tossing everything in a food processor for chopping or mincing, then adding the yogurt cheese and pulsing to blend.

Per 1/4 cup: Calories 45; protein 5 gm; carbohydrates 5 gm; fat <1 gm; cholesterol 0 mg; calcium 151 mg; sodium 134 mg. Exchanges: 1/2 skim milk.

Spinach-Onion Spread

Best served on a very flat crispy bread or toasted pita bread.

1 medium onion, minced
2 tablespoons light margarine
1 package (10 oz.) frozen chopped spinach
$1/2$ cup non-fat yogurt cheese
1 clove garlic, minced
1 tablespoon lemon juice, or more to taste
$1/8$ teaspoon salt, or to taste
  Black pepper to taste

Saute the onion in the margarine until softened.

Cook spinach according to package directions and squeeze out excess liquid. Chop finely.

In a medium-size bowl, whisk the yogurt cheese, garlic, lemon juice, salt and pepper until well blended and smooth. Stir in the onion and spinach. Cover and chill until serving time.

Makes about $1^1/2$ cups.

• *Food processor.* Combine all ingredients in the work bowl (using metal blade) and pulse to combine.

Per 1/4 cup: Calories 47; protein 3 gm; carbohydrates 5 gm; fat 2 gm; cholesterol 0 mg; calcium 116 mg; sodium 137 mg. Exchanges: 1/2 lowfat milk.

Hungarian Poppy Seed Cheese

*The Hungarian flavoring seems to cry out
for rye and pumpernickel crackers or bread.*

1 cup non-fat yogurt cheese
1 medium garlic clove, minced
1 tablespoon finely minced onion
2 teaspoons paprika
1 teaspoon poppy seeds
 Dash ground white pepper
 Salt, optional

In a medium-size bowl, combine all ingredients and blend well with a wire whisk. Cover and chill several hours or overnight.

Makes about 1 cup.

Per 1/4 cup: Calories 49; protein 5 gm; carbohydrates 5 gm; fat 1 gm; cholesterol 0 mg; calcium 154 mg; sodium 41 mg. Exchanges: 1/2 skim milk.

Viennese Liptauer

An Austrian specialty.

  1 anchovy fillet
¹/₂ teaspoon drained capers
¹/₂ tablespoon finely chopped onion
¹/₂ tablespoon Dijon-style mustard
³/₄ teaspoon paprika
  1 teaspoon caraway seeds
³/₄ cup non-fat yogurt cheese

   Mash the anchovy and capers with a fork in a medium-size bowl. Stir in the onion, mustard, paprika and caraway seeds. Add the yogurt cheese and whisk until smooth and well blended. Cover and chill several hours or overnight, to blend the flavors.
   Serve at room temperature. Particularly good with rye and pumpernickel rounds and small chunks of raw cabbage.
   Makes about ³/₄ cup.

Per 1/4 cup: Calories 50; protein 5 gm; carbohydrates 5 gm; fat <1 gm; cholesterol 0 mg; calcium 153 mg; sodium 132 mg. Exchanges: 1/2 skim milk.

Clam Dip

Guilt-free version of a traditional favorite.

2 cups non-fat yogurt cheese
1 clove garlic, minced
$1/2$ teaspoon ground red pepper (cayenne)
1 can ($6^1/2$ oz.) minced clams, well drained
$1/4$ cup diced pimiento, well drained
$1/4$ cup finely chopped green onion

In a medium-size bowl, whisk the yogurt cheese with garlic and red pepper until smooth. Add remaining ingredients and blend well. Cover and chill until serving time.

Makes about $2^1/4$ cups.

Per 1/4 cup: Calories 50; protein 6 gm; carbohydrates 5 gm; fat <1 gm; cholesterol 16 mg; calcium 138 mg; sodium 36 mg. Exchanges: 1/2 skim milk.

Gefilte Fish Spread

1 jar (12 oz.) gefilte fish
³/₄ cup non-fat yogurt cheese
1¹/₂ tablespoons prepared horseradish
³/₄ teaspoon lemon juice
   Dash black pepper

Drain fish, reserving the broth.

In a food processor (metal blade), process the fish until smooth. Add the remaining ingredients and pulse until mixed well. Thin with a little reserved broth, if desired. Cover and chill until serving time. Good with matzos or water crackers.

Makes about 2 cups.

Per 1/4 cup: Calories 51; protein 6 gm; carbohydrates 5 gm; fat 1 gm; cholesterol 12 mg; calcium 64 mg; sodium 238 mg. Exchanges: 1/2 skim milk.

Diet note: Not recommended for those on low-sodium diets.

Hot Crab Dip

Long forbidden by high fat, a favorite now brought up-to-date.

1 cup non-fat yogurt cheese
1 small clove garlic, minced
1 tablespoon lemon juice
1 tablespoon Dijon-style mustard
2 teaspoons white wine Worcestershire sauce
   Dash ground red pepper (cayenne)
6 ounces cooked crab meat, flaked

Combine the yogurt cheese, garlic, lemon juice, mustard, Worcestershire sauce and red pepper in a medium-size bowl and whisk until smooth. Stir in crab meat. Transfer to a saucepan and heat gently but do not boil.

Serve at once, with crackers or with small cubes of French bread on toothpicks.

Makes about 1 1/2 cups.

Per 1/4 cup: Calories 58; protein 8 gm; carbohydrates 4 gm; fat 1 gm; cholesterol 28 mg; calcium 111 mg; sodium 135 mg. Exchanges: 1 lean meat.

Diet note: Although crab is higher in cholesterol than most seafoods, its low fat content makes it acceptable for occasional use. To lower cholesterol, those not on a sodium-restricted diet may substitute artificial crab meat.

Shrimp Dip

This is good with crisp raw vegetables.

1 cup non-fat yogurt cheese
1 tablespoon Dijon-style mustard
2 teaspoons white wine Worcestershire sauce
2 teaspoons lemon juice
8 ounces tiny cooked shrimp (peeled), or 2 cans
   (4$\frac{1}{2}$ oz. *each*) tiny shrimp, rinsed and drained
$\frac{1}{2}$ cup finely chopped celery

   In a medium-sized bowl whisk the yogurt cheese, mustard, Worcestershire sauce and lemon juice until smooth. Add the shrimp and celery and mix well. (For a less chunky texture, chop or crumble the shrimp.) Cover and chill until serving time.
   Makes about 1$\frac{3}{4}$ cups.

Per 1/4 cup: Calories 59; protein 9 gm; carbohydrates 4 gm; fat 1 gm; cholesterol 45 mg; calcium 108 mg; sodium 118 mg. Exchanges: 1 lean meat.

Diet note: Although shrimp is higher in cholesterol than most seafoods, its low fat content makes it acceptable for occasional use. To lower cholesterol, other fresh fish (such as salmon, scallops or snapper) may be substituted; those not on a sodium-restricted diet may substitute artificial lobster meat.

Lima Bean Spread

Thin with water for a wonderful soup.

1 package (10 oz.) frozen baby lima beans
1⅓ cups non-fat yogurt cheese
1 tablespoon finely minced onion
1 teaspoon lemon juice
¼ teaspoon salt, or to taste
4 drops Tabasco sauce
  Dash black pepper
2 tablespoons chopped fresh parsley, garnish

Cook the lima beans according to package directions, about 20 minutes. Drain.

Transfer to a food processor (metal blade) and puree. Add remaining ingredients and pulse until well blended. Cover and chill until serving time. Sprinkle with chopped parsley just before serving.

Makes about 2¼ cups.

Per 1/4 cup: Calories 62; protein 5 gm; carbohydrates 10 gm; fat <1 gm; cholesterol 0 mg; calcium 95 mg; sodium 91 mg. Exchanges: 1 vegetable and 1/2 skim milk.

Tuna Pate

1   can (6½ oz.) water-packed tuna (no salt added)
½   cup non-fat yogurt cheese
1   tablespoon chili sauce
1   tablespoon finely chopped fresh parsley
1   tablespoon minced onion
⅛   teaspoon Tabasco sauce

Drain the tuna and flake with a fork.

In a medium-size bowl, combine the yogurt cheese, chili sauce, parsley, onion and Tabasco and whisk until well blended. Stir in the tuna. Cover and chill until serving time.

Makes about 1⅛ cups.

Per 1/4 cup: Calories 63; protein 12 gm; carbohydrates 2 gm; fat <1 gm; cholesterol 14 mg; calcium 64 mg; sodium 149 mg. Exchanges: 1 lean meat.

Water Chestnut Dip

Good to nibble on when you're stir-frying.

2 cups non-fat yogurt cheese
2 tablespoons instant beef bouillon granules (low-sodium)
$1/2$ teaspoon white wine Worcestershire sauce
1 clove garlic, minced
1 can (8 oz.) water chestnuts, drained and finely chopped
2 tablespoons diced pimientos, drained
1 tablespoon thinly sliced green onion
    Diced pimiento and chopped parsley, garnish

In a medium-size bowl, whisk yogurt cheese with the beef bouillon, Worcestershire sauce and minced garlic until smooth and well blended. Stir in the remaining ingredients. Cover and chill until serving time.

To serve, garnish with diced pimiento and chopped parsley, and surround with raw vegetables.

Makes about 2 cups.

Per 1/4 cup: Calories 65; protein 5 gm; carbohydrates 10 gm; fat <1 gm; cholesterol 0 mg; calcium 143 mg; sodium 53 mg. Exchanges: 1 vegetable and 1/2 skim milk.

Curried Shrimp Spread

 1/2 cup non-fat yogurt cheese
 1 tablespoon lemon juice
 1 tablespoon Major Grey's chutney
 1/2 teaspoon curry powder
 1 can (4 1/2 oz.) shrimp, drained and crumbled

In a medium-size bowl, whisk yogurt cheese, lemon juice, chutney and curry powder until well blended. Stir in the shrimp and mix well. Cover and chill until serving time.
Makes about 1 cup.

Per 1/4 cup: Calories 69; protein 10 gm; carbohydrates 5 gm; fat <1 gm; cholesterol 48 mg; calcium 109 mg; sodium 71 mg. Exchanges: 1 lean meat.

Diet note: Sodium can be lowered by substituting cooked, chopped fresh shrimp. Although shrimp is higher in cholesterol than most seafoods, its low fat content makes it acceptable for occasional use. To lower cholesterol, other fresh fish (such as salmon, scallops or snapper) may be substituted; those not on a sodium-restricted diet may substitute artificial lobster meat.

• *Easy Curry Spread.* Combine yogurt cheese with curry powder to taste. Place in serving dish. Spoon chutney over the top. Yummy!

Parsley Cheese

1 cup non-fat yogurt cheese
1/3 cup celery, minced (1 stalk)
1/4 cup minced onion (1/2 small onion)
2 tablespoons grated Parmesan cheese
2 tablespoons chunky peanut butter
2 tablespoons minced fresh parsley
2 tablespoons minced green pepper
1/2 teaspoon Tabasco sauce
1/2 teaspoon Dijon-style mustard
1/4 teaspoon celery seed
1/4 teaspoon paprika

Combine all ingredients in a large bowl and whisk until well blended. Cover and chill until serving time.

Serve as a spread or as a filling for cherry tomatoes, mushrooms or hollowed-out cucumber chunks.

Makes about 1 1/2 cups.

Per 1/4 cup: Calories 71; protein 5 gm; carbohydrates 5 gm; fat 3 gm; cholesterol 1 mg; calcium 125 mg; sodium 87 mg. Exchanges: 1/2 lowfat milk.

Diet note: To lower sodium, unsalted peanut butter may be used and the amount of Parmesan cheese may be reduced.

Hot Mushroom Dip

1 pound mushrooms, sliced
1/4 cup chopped onion
3 tablespoons light margarine
2 tablespoons flour
2 tablespoons dry white wine
1 cup non-fat yogurt cheese

Saute mushrooms and onion in margarine until golden. Add flour and mix well as the mixture continues to cook. Add the wine and continue stirring until mixture thickens.

Remove from heat, stir in yogurt cheese, and serve.

(May be refrigerated and reheated over low heat just before serving.)

Makes about 1³/₄ cups.

Per 1/4 cup: Calories 73; protein 4 gm; carbohydrates 8 gm; fat 3 gm; cholesterol 0 mg; calcium 87 mg; sodium 84 mg. Exchanges: 1/2 lowfat milk.

Caviar Dip

A very festive dip - save for special occasions!

2 cups non-fat yogurt cheese
1 teaspoon white wine Worcestershire sauce
$1/2$ teaspoon fresh lemon juice
$1/4$ teaspoon ground red pepper (cayenne)
1 jar (4 oz.) caviar
$1/4$ cup finely minced onion

In a medium-size bowl, whisk yogurt cheese with Worcestershire sauce, lemon juice and red pepper until smooth. Gently stir in the caviar. Cover and chill until serving time.

Just before serving, fold in the minced onion.

Serve with melba toast rounds, cocktail-size rye or pumpernickel bread and fresh vegetables.

Makes about 2 cups.

Per 1/8 cup: Calories 40; protein 4 gm; carbohydrates 5 gm; fat 1 gm; cholesterol 21 mg; calcium 91 mg; sodium 178 mg. Exchanges: 1/2 skim milk.

Diet note: Although caviar is high in cholesterol and sodium, combining it with yogurt cheese will allow you to experience the flavor of caviar while lowering these values.

Garlic-Cheese Spread

6 large cloves garlic, minced
1/2 teaspoon dried Italian herbs
1/4 teaspoon freshly ground black pepper
1 tablespoon olive oil
1 1/2 cups non-fat yogurt cheese
1/4 cup grated Parmesan cheese
1 tablespoon snipped chives

Saute garlic, herbs, and pepper in olive oil until the garlic browns lightly. Drain off any oil. Combine with remaining ingredients in a medium-size bowl, and whisk together until well blended. Chill until serving time.

Serve as a spread, or fill hollowed-out cherry tomatoes or celery sticks.

Makes about 1 1/2 cups.

• *Variation.* For an entree, fill cooked pasta shells or other large pasta with Garlic-Cheese Spread, place in a shallow baking dish, and top with a good tomato sauce. Bake in a medium oven until hot.

Per 1/4 cup: Calories 81; protein 6 gm; carbohydrates 6 gm; fat 3 gm; cholesterol 2 mg; calcium 195 mg; sodium 84 mg. Exchanges: 1/2 skim milk and 1 fat.

Mushroom Spread

Thin with chicken stock to make a dip.

$^{1}/_{2}$ cup chopped onion
$^{1}/_{2}$ pound mushrooms, sliced
$^{1}/_{3}$ cup port wine
    Salt and pepper, optional
$^{1}/_{2}$ cup (2 oz.) grated sharp Cheddar cheese
$^{2}/_{3}$ cup non-fat yogurt cheese

Microwave the onion, covered, for 30 seconds to soften (or saute in 2 tablespoons light margarine over moderate heat until soft). Transfer to a skillet, add mushrooms and port and cook until the mushrooms are soft and the liquid has evaporated. Season to taste and allow to cool.

In a food processor (metal blade), process grated Cheddar and yogurt cheese until very smooth, scraping down the sides of the work bowl. Add mushroom mixture and pulse several times until it is pureed.

Makes about 1$^{1}/_{4}$ cup.

1/4 cup: Calories 109; protein 6 gm; carbohydrates 6 gm; fat 4 gm; cholesterol 12 mg; calcium 163 mg; sodium 93 mg. Exchanges: 1 vegetable, 1/2 skim milk and 1 fat.

Diet note: Low-fat and/or low-sodium Cheddar may be substituted, although the flavor will be milder.

Pesto Spread

Versatile and delicious!

²/₃ cup fresh basil leaves
¹/₃ cup fresh flat-leaf parsley
4 medium cloves garlic
¹/₃ cup pine nuts
¹/₂ cup (1³/₄ oz.) freshly grated Parmesan cheese
1 cup non-fat yogurt cheese
¹/₂ teaspoon freshly ground black pepper

Combine basil, parsley and garlic cloves in a food processor (metal blade) and process until fine. Add the pine nuts and Parmesan cheese, and process until the pine nuts are finely chopped. Add the yogurt cheese and pepper, and pulse until well blended. Cover and chill until serving time.
Makes about 1¹/₃ cups.

Per 1/4 cup: Calories 110; protein 8 gm; carbohydrates 8 gm; fat 5 gm; cholesterol 6 mg; calcium 314 mg; sodium 142 mg. Exchanges: 1 medium fat meat and 1 vegetable.

• **Pesto Pasta Sauce.** Mix Pesto Spread with hot pasta and sprinkle with additional Parmesan.

• **Pesto Salad Dressing.** Add 1 part vinegar to 2 parts Pesto Spread.

Blue Cheese Spread

Stuff celery sticks and serve before dinner.
Serve with apple or pear slices for dessert.

1 cup non-fat yogurt cheese
1 package (4 oz.) blue cheese
$1/2$ cup minced fresh parsley
1 tablespoon brandy or cognac
1-2 teaspoons poppy seeds, optional garnish
   Sliced black olives, optional garnish

In a medium-size bowl, whisk the yogurt cheese and blue cheese until fluffy. Stir in the parsley and brandy and mix well. Cover and chill until serving time.

Garnish with poppy seeds and black olive slices if desired.

Makes about $1^1/4$ cups.

Per 1/4 cup: Calories 121; protein 9 gm; carbohydrates 4 gm; fat 7 gm; cholesterol 17 mg; calcium 240 mg; sodium 351 mg. Exchanges: 1 high-fat meat and 1 vegetable.

Diet note: Although blue cheese is high in fat, cholesterol and sodium, combining it with yogurt cheese gives the full flavor while lowering these values. Not recommended for those on low-sodium diets.

• **Variation.** For blue cheese salad dressing, omit brandy, and thin to desired consistency with water or skim milk.

Curry-Cheese Ball

1 cup non-fat yogurt cheese
1 cup (4 oz.) medium sharp Cheddar cheese, grated
⅓ cup (about 1½ oz.) chopped pecans
1-2 cloves garlic, minced
    Curry powder

Combine the yogurt cheese, Cheddar cheese, pecans and garlic, and form into a ball. Refrigerate.

Just before serving, roll in curry powder, or press the curry powder into the cheese, so that the entire surface is coated.

Makes about 1½ cups.

Per 1/4 cup: Calories 143; protein 8 gm; carbohydrates 4 gm; fat 10 gm; cholesterol 20 mg; calcium 233 mg; sodium 144 mg. Exchanges: 1 high-fat meat and 1/2 skim milk.

Diet note: Although Cheddar cheese is high in fat and cholesterol, and pecans are high in fat, combining them with yogurt cheese gives the full flavor while lowering these values. To lower them further, reduce amount of Cheddar and pecans; low-fat and/or low-sodium Cheddar may also be substituted, although the flavor will be milder.

Cheddar-Chutney Spread

The flavor is straight from Bombay.

1 cup non-fat yogurt cheese
2 cups (8 oz.) sharp Cheddar cheese, grated
$\frac{1}{2}$ cup Major Grey's chutney
1 tablespoon curry powder, or to taste
1 teaspoon ground ginger

Combine all ingredients in a food processor (metal blade) and process until smooth. Cover and chill until serving time.
Serve with melba rounds and assorted crackers.
Makes about 2 cups.

Per 1/8 cup: Calories 89; protein 5 gm; carbohydrates 5 gm; fat 5 gm; cholesterol 15 mg; calcium 142 mg; sodium 111 mg. Exchanges: 1/2 skim milk and 1 fat.

Diet note: Although Cheddar cheese is high in fat, cholesterol and sodium, combining it with yogurt cheese gives the full flavor while lowering these values. Low-fat and/or low-sodium Cheddar may also be substituted, although the flavor will be milder.

2 • APPETIZERS

Appetizers frequently mean parties, but parties are difficult because almost everyone is on a diet of some sort.

When you're invited to a party and you aren't sure if there will be anything you can eat (without guilt), it's possible to plan ahead and take something with you. Your hostess won't turn down an extra dish offered graciously; say you just whipped up something interesting and wanted to share it. (While you're at it, it would be a nice touch to take the recipe along.)

If you're the host or hostess, it's considerate to provide several low-fat, low-cal choices, clearly indicated. You can either arrange them together or mark each one with a small card. Your guests will love you and you'll have something you can enjoy, too!

The appetizers in this chapter are good party fare. They can be quickly and easily prepared. Many can be made ahead. As before, the recipes are arranged by calories, from lowest to highest.

The best part of a party, of course, is snacking on those wonderful leftovers the next day. These recipes will make it possible.

Stuffed Mushrooms

The filling can also be used as a spread.

1 pound medium-size mushrooms
2 tablespoons light margarine
1 cup non-fat yogurt cheese
⅓ cup grated Parmesan cheese
2 tablespoons chopped green onion

Remove stems from mushrooms and saute the mushroom caps in margarine for 3 or 4 minutes to soften (or microwave, covered, for 1 to 2 minutes).

In a medium-size bowl, combine yogurt cheese and Parmesan cheese, and whisk until well blended and smooth. Chop mushroom stems to measure 1/2 cup, and stir into cheese mixture with the green onions. (If desired, the chopped stems may be cooked, and cooled slightly, before adding to the cheese).

Fill each mushroom cap with about one-half tablespoon of the mixture.

Makes about 30.

2 mushrooms: Calories 33; protein 3 gm; carbohydrates 3 gm; fat 1 gm; cholesterol 1 mg; calcium 64 mg; sodium 52 mg. Exchanges: 1 vegetable.

Stuffed Snow Peas

You can use many of the spreads in this book to
stuff snow peas. Use your imagination!

25 snow peas (Chinese pea pods)
 1 cup non-fat yogurt cheese
 1 teaspoon coarse-grained Dijon-style mustard
    Salt, optional
    Freshly ground black pepper to taste
¼ cup finely chopped pecans

Remove ends and strings from snow peas.

The snow peas may be raw or blanched. To blanch them, immerse in boiling water for 10 seconds, then plunge into cold water; when cool, drain and pat dry.

In a medium-size bowl, combine yogurt cheese, mustard and seasonings; mix with a wire whisk until smooth and well blended. Using a sharp knife, slit each pea pod open along the straight side. Spoon 1 teaspoon of mixture into each pea pod (or pipe from a pastry bag).

Sprinkle nuts on the cheese edge of each pea pod. Cover and chill until serving time.

Makes 25 appetizers.

3 stuffed pea pods: Calories 45; protein 3 gm; carbohydrates 3 gm; fat 2 gm; cholesterol 0 mg; calcium 73 mg; sodium 27 mg. Exchanges: 1/2 skim milk.

Diet note: To lower fat and calories, omit the nuts.

Potato-Caviar Bites

A beautiful and delicious hors d'oeuvre. Sweet potato slices are topped with shimmering caviar over yogurt cheese.

2 2-inch diameter sweet potatoes (about 1 lb.)
$1/2$ cup non-fat yogurt cheese
1 ounce caviar

Peel the potatoes and cut into rounds about 1/4-inch thick. Steam or microwave until just done. Drain and pat dry. Cool. Arrange on a serving platter.

In a small bowl, whisk yogurt cheese until smooth. Place about 1/2 teaspoon in the center of each potato slice, then top with about 1/8 teaspoon caviar.

Makes about 40 pieces.

Per 2 pieces: Calories 31; protein 1 gm; carbohydrates 6 gm; fat <1 gm; cholesterol 4 mg; calcium 24 mg; sodium 37 mg. Exchanges: 1 vegetable.

• **Variation.** Substitute unpeeled cucumber rounds or tiny red potatoes, cooked and partially hollowed out, for the sweet potatoes.

Spinach Cheese Bites

. . . like little souffles.

1 package (10 oz.) frozen chopped spinach, thawed
3 green onions, minced
1 tablespoon light margarine
1 cup non-fat yogurt cheese
¼ cup freshly grated Parmesan cheese
2 egg whites
3 tablespoons minced fresh parsley
1 clove garlic, minced, optional
  Salt, optional
  Pepper and nutmeg to taste

Preheat oven to 350°. Spray 16 miniature muffin cups with non-stick cooking spray.

Drain spinach well, squeezing out as much liquid as possible. Chop finely. Saute the green onion in the margarine until softened.

In a modium cizo bowl, whick yogurt chooco, Parmocan cheese and egg whites until smooth. Blend in spinach, green onions, parsley, garlic and seasonings. Mix well.

Spoon into the muffin cups and bake until golden, about 25 to 30 minutes.

Makes 16 appetizers.

2 appetizers: Calories 54; protein 5 gm; carbohydrates 5 gm; fat 2 gm; cholesterol 2 mg; calcium 162 mg; sodium 113 mg. Exchanges: 1/2 lowfat milk.

Barbecued Chicken Appetizers

An excellent way to use leftover chicken.

$^1/_2$ cup non-fat yogurt cheese
$^1/_2$ tablespoon barbecue sauce
  Dash Tabasco sauce
 1 cup minced barbecued chicken (1 small breast)
24 melba toast rounds

In a medium-size bowl, whisk yogurt cheese with barbecue sauce and Tabasco sauce until smooth. Blend in the chicken.

To serve, pipe or spread onto melba rounds (about 2 teaspoons each).

Makes 24 appetizers.

3 melba rounds with spread: Calories 59; protein 5 gm; carbohydrates 6 gm; fat 1 gm; cholesterol 10 mg; calcium 37 mg; sodium 95 mg. Exchange: 1/2 low fat milk.

Herb Cheesecake

2 cups non-fat yogurt cheese
$^1/_4$ cup grated Parmesan cheese
3 cloves garlic, minced
$1^1/_2$ tablespoons dried basil, or 1 cup chopped
   fresh basil, firmly-packed
   Pinch black pepper
4 egg whites, slightly beaten

Preheat oven to 325°. Spray an 8-inch pie pan or 7-inch springform pan with non-stick cooking spray.

In a medium-size bowl, whisk yogurt cheese with Parmesan cheese, garlic, basil and pepper until well blended. Stir in the egg whites and mix well.

Pour into the pan and smooth the top with a spatula. Bake until the center is set: 25 to 30 minutes for a pie pan, or 55 to 60 minutes for a springform. Cool slightly on a wire rack, then refrigerate until chilled.

Serve whole, sliced into 16 wedges, or allow your guests to slice small wedges to eat with fruit or crackers.

Per wedge: Calories 31; protein 4 gm; carbohydrates 3 gm; fat <1 gm; cholesterol 1 mg; calcium 97 mg; sodium 49 mg. Exchanges: 1/2 skim milk.

Salmon Stuffed Tomatoes

You can make this in no time with a food processor.

15 cherry tomatoes
$^1/_3$ cup non-fat yogurt cheese
  1 tablespoon dry sherry
  1 tablespoon lemon juice
  1 tablespoon snipped fresh dill
     Salt and pepper, optional
  1 cup cooked, flaked salmon
     Fresh dill sprigs, garnish

Cut the tops off the tomatoes and gently squeeze out the seeds. Invert on paper towels and let drain for 20 minutes.

In a medium-size bowl, combine yogurt cheese, sherry, lemon juice, dill, salt and pepper, and whisk until blended. Stir in the salmon, mixing well until smooth.

Fill each tomato with about one-half tablespoon of puree. Garnish with small sprigs of dill. Chill before serving.

Makes 15 appetizers.

1 stuffed tomato: Calories 32; protein 4 gm; carbohydrates 2 gm; fat 1 gm; cholesterol 6 mg; calcium 17 mg; sodium 20 mg. Exchanges: 1 vegetable.

Chicken Skewers

The marinade also makes a good basting sauce.
Use for lamb and turkey as well as for chicken.

1 pound chicken tenders* (about 10)
$^2/_3$ cup non-fat yogurt cheese
4 small cloves garlic, finely minced
1 tablespoon finely minced onion
2 teaspoons grated fresh gingeroot
1 teaspoon *each* turmeric and ground coriander
1 teaspoon dried red pepper flakes
$^1/_2$ teaspoon ground cumin

Cut each fillet in half to make 2 pieces (about 1 x 3 inches).

Combine remaining ingredients in a medium-size bowl and blend well with a wire whisk. Add chicken, and stir to coat evenly. Cover and allow to marinate in the refrigerator for at least 1 hour.

Thread chicken pieces on small skewers and cook on a prepared grill (about 4 inches away from coals) until done, about 3 to 4 minutes per side. Chicken will be done when it loses its pinkness and is firm to the touch.

Makes 20 skewers.

* A chicken tender is the small piece of meat attached to the underside of a boned chicken breast. Cubes of chicken breast may be substituted.

2 skewers: Calories 77; protein 9 gm; carbohydrates 2 gm; fat 3 gm; cholesterol 23 mg; calcium 47 mg; sodium 34 mg. Exchanges: 1 lean meat and 1 vegetable.

Spinach-Cheese Squares

 $^1/_4$ cup light margarine

 2 packages (10 oz. *each*) frozen chopped spinach, thawed

 4 egg whites

 1 cup non-fat yogurt cheese

 1 clove garlic, minced

 $^3/_4$ cup all-purpose flour

 1 teaspoon baking powder

 $^1/_4$ teaspoon salt, or to taste

 2 cups ($^1/_2$ lb.) grated Monterey Jack or Swiss cheese

Preheat oven to 350°. Place margarine in a 9 x 13-inch baking pan and set in oven until melted. Remove from oven.

Drain the spinach well, squeezing out as much liquid as possible.

In a large bowl, combine the egg whites, yogurt cheese and garlic, and whisk until smooth. Add flour, baking powder and salt, and mix well. Blend in the Monterey Jack cheese and spinach. Spread evenly in the baking pan.

Bake for 35 minutes or until golden. Cool for 30 minutes, then cut into 1 1/2-inch squares. Serve warm or cold.

Makes 48 squares.

Per square: Calories 37; protein 3 gm; carbohydrates 3 gm; fat 2 gm; cholesterol 4 mg; calcium 81 mg; sodium 60 mg. Exchanges: 1/2 medium fat meat.

Diet note: Although cheese is high in fat and cholesterol, combining it with yogurt cheese gives full flavor while lowering these values. Also, the amount of cheese may be reduced, or low-fat and/or low-sodium cheese may be substituted, although the flavor will be milder.

Artichoke and Green Chile Pie

Good with Baked Corn Chips.

1 cup non-fat yogurt cheese
1¹/₂ cups (5¹/₄ oz.) grated Parmesan cheese
2 large cloves garlic, minced
¹/₄ teaspoon dried red pepper flakes
1 can (14 oz.) artichoke hearts (water-packed), drained
1 can (4 oz.) diced green chiles, drained
¹/₃ cup finely chopped red bell pepper

Preheat oven to 350°. Spray an 8-inch pie pan or 7-inch springform pan with non-stick cooking spray.

In a medium-size bowl, combine the yogurt cheese with the Parmesan cheese, garlic and red pepper flakes, and whisk until well blended. Chop artichoke hearts and stir into cheese mixture with chiles and bell pepper.

Spoon mixture into the pan. Bake until golden brown, about 25 to 35 minutes. Serve hot or cold, as a spread, a first course or a vegetable side dish.

Cut into 16 wedges.

- *Variation.* For a dip, serve unbaked, accompanied by Baked Corn Chips *(recipe, page 138).*

Per wedge: Calories 58; protein 6 gm; carbohydrates 4 gm; fat 3 gm; cholesterol 6 mg; calcium 153 mg; sodium 231 mg. Exchanges: 1/2 lowfat milk.

Diet note: Not recommended for low-sodium diets.

Crab Appetizer

An easy make-ahead party dish!

1½ cups non-fat yogurt cheese
1 small clove garlic, minced
¼ teaspoon white wine Worcestershire sauce
8 ounces crab meat, flaked
½ cup chili sauce (may substitute seafood cocktail sauce)
¼ cup chopped fresh parsley

In a medium-size bowl, whisk together the yogurt cheese, garlic and Worcestershire sauce until well blended. Spread into an 8-inch circle on a serving dish. Cover evenly with the crab. Cover and chill several hours or overnight.

Just before serving, stir the chili sauce and spread over the crab, then sprinkle with the chopped parsley.

Serve with crackers or melba toast rounds.

Serves 12 generously.

Per 1/4 cup: Calories 61; protein 9 gm; carbohydrates 4 gm; fat 1 gm; cholesterol 28 mg; calcium 122 mg; sodium 95 mg. Exchanges: 1 lean meat.

Diet note: Although crab is higher in cholesterol than most seafoods, its low fat content makes it acceptable for occasional use. To reduce cholesterol, other fresh fish (such as sole or scallops) may be substituted; those not on a sodium-restricted diet may substitute artificial crab meat.

Fiesta Puffs

These are quicker to make than you'd think.

1 pound ground turkey
2 cloves garlic, minced
1½ teaspoons *each* ground cumin and chili powder
½ teaspoon salt, or to taste
1 cup non-fat yogurt cheese
2 tablespoons medium-hot taco sauce
¾ cup coarsely crushed tortillas or corn chips
¼ cup chopped black olives
½ cup (2 oz.) grated mild Cheddar cheese

Preheat over to 425°. Spray 30 miniature muffin cups with non-stick cooking spray.

Combine turkey, garlic, cumin, chile powder and salt, and blend well. Place 2 teaspoons of this mixture into each muffin cup and press into the bottom and sides to form a shell.

In a medium-size bowl, whisk the yogurt cheese and taco sauce until smooth. Stir in tortillas and olives. Spoon 1 heaping teaspoon into each shell. Sprinkle the tops with a little Cheddar cheese.

Bake 8 to 10 minutes, until the meat is cooked and the cheese is melted.

Makes 30 appetizers.

Per puff: Calories 62; protein 5 gm; carbohydrates 2 gm; fat 3 gm; cholesterol 12 mg; calcium 43 mg; sodium 65 mg. Exchanges: 1 lean meat.

Diet note: Reduce fat and calories by using Baked Corn Chips *(recipe, page 138).* Cheddar cheese is high in fat and cholesterol; combining it with yogurt cheese gives the full flavor while lowering these values. Low-fat and/or low-sodium Cheddar may also be substituted, although the flavor will be milder.

Stuffed Banana Chiles

1 cup (4 oz.) grated sharp Cheddar cheese
$1/2$ cup non-fat yogurt cheese
2 teaspoons lemon juice
$1/2$ teaspoon instant chicken bouillon powder (low-sodium)
 Tabasco sauce to taste
$1/2$ medium tomato, seeded and quartered
2 tablespoons coarsely chopped onion
2 ounces ($1/2$ can) diced green chiles, drained
9 banana chiles (sweet long yellow chiles)

For the filling (may use food processor), combine Cheddar cheese, yogurt cheese, lemon juice, bouillon powder and Tabasco in a medium-size bowl; blend with wire whisk. Finely chop the tomato and onion; add with the diced chiles, stirring until well mixed. Cover and chill until ready to use.

Char banana chiles over a gas flame or in the broiler until blackened on all sides. Place in a paper bag and let stand 10 minutes to steam. Peel the chiles.

Using a small sharp knife, slit chiles open on one long side. Cut off stems and remove the seeds. Rinse if necessary and pat dry. Open flat, inside facing up, and spread evenly with filling.

Starting at one long side, roll up, enclosing filling completely. Cover and chill at least 2 hours before serving. Garnish if desired with a sprig of fresh herbs at the stem end.

Makes 9 appetizers.

Per appetizer: Calories 71; protein 5 gm; carbohydrates 4 gm; fat 4 gm; cholesterol 13 mg; calcium 126 mg; sodium 182 mg. Exchanges: 1 vegetable and 1 fat.

Diet note: Although Cheddar cheese is high in fat and cholesterol, combining it with yogurt cheese gives the full flavor while lowering these values. Low-fat and/or low-sodium Cheddar may also be substituted, although the flavor will be milder.

Tex-Mex Cheesecake

For an appetizer with a Mexican accent.

2 cups non-fat yogurt cheese
4 egg whites
1 tablespoon cornstarch
1 cup canned yellow corn (no salt added), drained
1 large clove garlic, finely minced
2 tablespoons diced green chiles (canned)
1/4 cup sliced black olives
   Pepper and hot pepper sauce to taste

Preheat the oven to 325°. Spray an 8-inch pie pan or 7-inch springform pan with non-stick cooking spray.

In a large bowl, whisk yogurt cheese, egg whites and cornstarch until smooth. Add remaining ingredients and whisk well to combine.

Pour into pan and smooth the top with a spatula. Bake until center is set: 25 to 30 minutes for a pie pan, or 55 to 60 minutes for a springform. Cool slightly on a wire rack. Refrigerate until chilled.

Cut into 8 wedges.

Per wedge: Calories 75; protein 7 gm; carbohydrates 9 gm; fat 1 gm; cholesterol 0 mg; calcium 148 mg; sodium 101 mg. Exchanges: 1 vegetable and 1/2 skim milk.

Diet note: To lower calories and sodium, reduce or omit black olives.

Quiche Squares

    6 egg whites
$^1/_2$ cup + 2 tablespoons all-purpose flour
    1 teaspoon baking powder
    1 cup + 2 tablespoons non-fat yogurt cheese
$1^1/_2$ cups (6 oz.) grated Monterey Jack cheese
    1 can (4 oz.) diced green chiles, drained

Preheat the oven to 350°. Spray an 8 x 8-inch baking pan with non-stick cooking spray.

In a large bowl, whisk egg whites until foamy. Add flour, baking powder and yogurt cheese and whisk until smooth. Fold in the Monterey Jack cheese and chiles.

Spread in the pan and bake for 30 to 35 minutes. Cool in pan 10 minutes. To serve, cut into 2-inch squares.

Makes 16 squares.

Per square: Calories 75; protein 6 gm; carbohydrates 5 gm; fat 3 gm; cholesterol 11 mg; calcium 138 mg; sodium 210 mg. Exchanges: 1 medium fat meat.

Diet note: Although Monterey Jack cheese is high in fat and cholesterol, combining it with yogurt cheese gives the full flavor while lowering these values. Low-fat and/or low-sodium cheese may be substituted, although the flavor will be milder.

Cucumber Tea Sandwiches

1 medium onion, finely chopped
1 cucumber, peeled, seeded and finely chopped
2 cups non-fat yogurt cheese
$^{1}/_{4}$ teasoon salt, or to taste
24 to 30 slices whole wheat bread*

Drain the onion and cucumber in a colander. Pat dry with towels, if necessary.

In a medium-size bowl, whisk the yogurt cheese and salt until smooth. Add vegetables and mix well. Cover and chill until serving time.

Trim the crusts from the bread. If you are not planning to make the sandwiches right away, cover well to keep fresh.

Just before serving, spread about 2 tablespoons of the mixture on each slice of bread. Cut diagonally into triangles.

Makes about 3 cups spread, for 48 to 60 sandwiches.

*Nutritional information on page 178.

Per 1/4 cup spread: Calories 30; protein 3 gm; carbohydrates 4 gm; fat tr ; cholesterol 0 mg; calcium 96 mg; sodium 73 mg. Exchanges: 1/2 skim milk.

Vegetable Cheese Pie

1 cup non-fat yogurt cheese
1 teaspoon lemon juice
$^1/_2$ teaspoon Worcestershire sauce
2 drops Tabasco sauce, or more to taste
   Dash paprika
$^1/_4$ cup finely chopped green pepper
$^1/_4$ cup finely chopped celery
2 tablespoons finely chopped onion
8 small pimiento-stuffed olives, chopped (2 Tbsp.)
$^2/_3$ cup cheese cracker crumbs

In a medium-size bowl, whisk yogurt cheese, lemon juice, Worcestershire sauce, Tabasco sauce and paprika until smooth. Stir in the green pepper, celery, onion and olives.

Line a 2-cup souffle dish with plastic wrap. Spread with half the cheese mixture; sprinkle with one-third of the crumbs. Repeat with a layer of cheese mixture then one-third of the crumbs. Cover and chill until serving time.

To serve, turn out on a platter, remove the plastic wrap and sprinkle with remaining crumbs. Cut into small wedges and surround with raw vegetables such as cucumbers, celery and carrot strps.

Makes about 1$^3/_4$ cups.

Per 1/4 cup: Calories 68; protein 4 gm; carbohydrates 8 gm; fat 2; cholesterol 0 mg; calcium 91 mg; sodium 188 mg. Exchanges: 1 vegetable and 1/2 skim milk.

Diet note: For low-sodium diets, omit part or all of the olives.

3 · HEARTY SNACKS

What do you nibble on when you watch TV?

Potato chips? Hot dogs? Pizza?

Think about the high calories, fat and cholesterol . . . .

Here are some other options that taste great and are good for you, too. Although they are arranged by calories including the suggested accompaniment (low to high), the nutritional analysis for both the sandwiches and stuffed potatoes is given for the filling or stuffing mixture alone.

A hearty snack can be eaten at any time and will also make a satisfying lunch or light supper dish. Hearty snacks are also good picnic foods.

Pocket Lasagne

This is very, very filling. Half can be a satisfying snack.

1 cup non-fat yogurt cheese
2 tablespoons tomato paste
½ small onion, minced
1 clove garlic, minced
½ tablespoon grated Parmesan cheese
½ tablespoon minced parsley
1 teaspoon dried mixed Italian herbs
  Salt, optional
4 5-inch rounds pita bread, split open
2 ounces part-skim mozzarella cheese

Combine the yogurt cheese, tomato paste, onion, garlic, Parmesan cheese, parsley and seasonings, and whisk well.

Spread about one-fourth cup of this mixture over the bottom of each round, and sprinkle with grated mozzarella. Broil until the cheese melts, about a minute or so; then replace tops, press together, and broil a few moments longer.

Makes about 1 cup, for 4 pocket lasagnes.

Per 1/2 lasagne: Calories 95; protein 7 gm; carbohydrates 15 gm; fat 1 gm; cholesterol 4 mg; calcium 81 mg; sodium 148 mg. Exchanges: 1/2 starch/bread and 1/2 skim milk.

Cheese Pizza

 2 tablespoons + 2 teaspoons light margarine
$^2/_3$ cup non-fat yogurt cheese
 4 egg whites
$^1/_2$ cup all-purpose flour
$^1/_4$ cup whole wheat flour
 1 teaspoon baking powder
$^1/_2$ cup tomato sauce (no salt added)
$^1/_2$ teaspoon *each* dried oregano and dried basil
 1 large clove garlic, minced
 4 ounces part-skim mozzarella cheese, grated
 1 tablespoon grated Parmesan cheese

Preheat the oven to 375°. Spray a 9- or 10-inch pie pan with non-stick cooking spray.

Melt margarine; when cool, combine with the yogurt cheese and egg whites in a medium-size bowl. Whisk until well mixed.

Combine the flours and baking powder, then whisk into the yogurt mixture. Spread on bottom and partly up the sides of the baking dish.

Combine tomato sauce, oregano, basil and garlic; spread evenly over the crust, leaving a 1/2-inch border around the edge. Sprinkle with mozzarella and Parmesan.

Bake 20 to 25 minutes.

Cool 5 minutes before cutting into 10 wedges.

Per wedge: Calories 96; protein 7 gm; carbohydrates 9 gm; fat 3 gm; cholesterol 7 mg; calcium 75 mg; sodium 168 mg. Exchanges: 1/2 starch/bread and 1 lean meat.

Garlic-Chive Stuffed Potatoes

Try the stuffing mixture as a dip.

1 cup non-fat yogurt cheese
1 small clove garlic, minced
1 tablespoon snipped fresh chives
$^1/_4$ teaspoon dried thyme
   Freshly ground black pepper, to taste
2 baked potatoes*

Place all topping ingredients in a medium-size bowl and whisk until smooth and well blended. Cover and chill until ready to use.

Slice each potato in half lengthwise, and fluff up the insides with a fork. Top each half with about one-fourth cup of the mixture.

Makes about 1 cup, for 4 potato halves.

*Nutritional information on page 182.

Per 1/4 cup mixture: Calories 41; protein 5 gm; carbohydrates 5 gm; fat tr; cholesterol 0 mg; calcium 143 mg; sodium 40 mg. Exchanges: 1/2 skim milk.

• **Variation.** Omit the thyme and add 1 to 4 tablespoons of freshly grated Parmesan cheese, to taste.

Broccoli-Cheese Stuffed Potatoes

Try the stuffing mixture as a sandwich filling.

1 package (10 oz.) frozen chopped broccoli
$^1/_3$ cup non-fat yogurt cheese
3 tablespoons grated Parmesan cheese
1 tablespoon fresh lemon juice
1 tablespoon Dijon-style mustard
3 hard-cooked egg whites, finely chopped
  Salt and pepper, optional
3 baked potatoes*

Cook the broccoli according to package directions. Drain, and press out excess liquid. Chop finely.

In a medium-size bowl, whisk together the yogurt cheese, Parmesan cheese, lemon juice and mustard until smooth. Blend in the broccoli, egg whites and seasonings. Cover and chill until ready to use.

Slice each potato in half lengthwise, and fluff up the insides with a fork. Top each half with about one-fourth cup of the mixture.

Makes about 1$^1/_2$ cups, for 6 potato halves.

*Nutritional information on page 182.

Per 1/4 cup mixture: Calories 44; protein 5 gm; carbohydrates 4 gm; fat 1 gm; cholesterol 2 mg; calcium 94 mg; sodium 110 mg. Exchanges: 1/2 skim milk.

Lemon-Chive Stuffed Potatoes

Try the stuffing mixture as a sauce for
cooked vegetables or cold poached fish.

1 cup non-fat yogurt cheese
2 tablespoons snipped fresh chives or green onion tops
1 medium clove garlic, minced
$1/2$ teaspoon grated lemon peel
$1/2$ large lemon, juiced
2 baked potatoes*

In a medium-size bowl, whisk all the topping ingredients together until well blended. Cover and chill until ready to use.

Slice each potato in half lengthwise, and fluff up the insides with a fork. Top each half with about one-fourth cup of the mixture.

Makes about 1 cup, for 4 potato halves.

*Nutritional information on page 182.

Per 1/4 cup mixture: Calories 46; protein 5 gm; carbohydrates 6 gm; fat tr; cholesterol 0 mg; calcium 145 mg; sodium 41 mg. Exchanges: 1/2 skim milk.

Zucchini Stuffed Potatoes

Try the stuffing mixture as a sauce for cooked vegetables.

1   cup non-fat yogurt cheese
3   tablespoons minced green onion
$^1/_8$ teaspoon salt, or to taste
1   small zucchini, grated
2   baked potatoes*

In a medium-size bowl, whisk yogurt cheese, green onions and salt until smooth and well blended. Stir in the zucchini. Cover and chill until ready to use.

Slice each potato in half lengthwise, and fluff up the insides with a fork. Top each half with about one-fourth cup of the mixture.

Makes about 1 cup, for 4 potato halves.

*Nutritional information on page 182.

Per 1/4 cup mixture: Calories 47; protein 5 gm; carbohydrates 6 gm; fat <1 gm; cholesterol 0 mg; calcium 148 mg; sodium 107 mg. Exchanges: 1/2 skim milk.

Chopped Olive Sandwiches

Try this mixture as a stuffing for hard-cooked egg whites.

1 cup non-fat yogurt cheese
1 can (4 oz.) chopped black olives, drained
$1/3$ cup finely minced green onion
   Dash ground red pepper (cayenne)
5 slices whole wheat bread*

Combine all spread ingredients in a medium-size bowl, and whisk until well blended. Use about one-fourth cup of the mixture for each sandwich.

Makes about $1^{1}/_4$ cups spread, to cover 5 open-face sandwiches.

*Nutritional information on page 178.

Per 1/4 spread: Calories 63; protein 4 gm; carbohydrates 4 gm; fat 3 gm; cholesterol 0 mg; calcium 135 mg; sodium 215 mg. Exchanges: 1/2 lowfat milk.

Diet note: Not recommended for low-sodium diets.

Crab Salad Sandwich Spread

Try the crab mixture as a stuffing for tomatoes,
artichokes or hard-cooked egg whites.

$1/3$ cup non-fat yogurt cheese
3 tablespoons minced onion
1 teaspoon lemon juice
$1/4$ teaspoon salt, optional
   Dash black pepper
8 oz. cooked crab, flaked, or finely chopped cooked shrimp
$1/2$ cup finely chopped celery
5 slices bread*

In a medium-size bowl, whisk the yogurt cheese, onion, lemon juice, salt and pepper until well blended. Stir in the crab and celery. Use about one-fourth cup for each sandwich.
   Makes about $1^{1}/_{4}$ cups, for 5 sandwiches.

*Nutritional information on page 178.

Per 1/4 cup spread: Calories 57; protein 9 gm; carbohydrates 2 gm; fat <1 gm; cholesterol 45 mg; calcium 63 mg; sodium 117 mg. Exchanges: 1 lean meat.

Diet note: Although crab is higher in cholesterol than most seafoods, its low fat content makes it acceptable for occasional use. To reduce cholesterol, other fresh fish (such as salmon, scallops or snapper) may be substituted for the crab; those not on a sodium-restricted diet may substitute artificial crab meat.

Tailgate Treats

No one will know it's not beef!

1   cup non-fat yogurt cheese
1   tablespoon instant beef bouillon granules (low-sodium)
2   ounces turkey smoked sausage, finely chopped
2   tablespoons finely minced onion
10   slices rye or pumpernickel cocktail-size bread*

In a medium-size bowl, whisk yogurt cheese and bouillon granules until smooth. Stir in sausage and onion. Spread each slice of bread with 2 tablespoons spread.

Makes about 1¼ cups, for 10 open-face sandwiches.

*Nutritional information on page 178.

Per 1/4 cup filling (makes 2 sandwiches): Calories 62; protein 6 gm; carbohydrates 5 gm; fat 2 gm; cholesterol 8 mg; calcium 115 mg; sodium 118 mg. Exchanges: 1 lowfat milk.

Italian Sandwiches

Try the filling mixture as a dip.

1 cup non-fat yogurt cheese
2 tablespoons freshly grated Parmesan cheese
1 small clove garlic, minced
$1/4$ teaspoon dried oregano
$1/2$ cup minced turkey ham or turkey salami
1 large tomato, juiced, seeded and finely chopped
   Pepper to taste
6 slices Italian bread*

    In a medium-size bowl, combine yogurt cheese, Parmesan cheese, garlic and oregano and whisk until smooth. Add turkey and tomato and blend well. Season to taste. Toast the bread and cover each slice with about one-fourth cup of the mixture.
    Makes about 1 $1/2$ cups, for 6 open-face sandwiches.

*Nutritional information page 178.

Per 1/4 cup spread: Calories 59; protein 7 gm; carbohydrates 4 gm; fat 1 gm; cholesterol 1 mg; calcium 121 mg; sodium 192 mg. Exchanges: 1 lean meat.

Diet note: Those on low-sodium diets may substitute cooked fresh turkey.

Basic Tuna Sandwich Spread

1 cup non-fat yogurt cheese
1 can (6$\frac{1}{2}$ oz.) water-packed tuna (no salt added)
  Chopped green onion, garnish

Drain the tuna. Place in a food processor with the yogurt cheese and process (metal blade) until smooth. Cover and chill until serving time.
  Just before serving, sprinkle with chopped green onion.
  Makes about 1$\frac{1}{3}$ cups.

Per 1/4 cup spread: Calories 67; protein 11 gm; carbohydrates 3 gm; fat <1 gm; cholesterol 12 mg; calcium 106 mg; sodium 140 mg. Exchanges: 1 lean meat.

• **Variations.** Other ingredients may be added to taste, such as celery, onion, relish, etc. May also be used as a substitute for tuna sauce in vitello tonnato.

Tempting Tuna Sandwiches

1$\frac{1}{2}$ cups non-fat yogurt cheese
2 teaspoons prepared horseradish
1 teaspoon Worcestershire sauce
1 can (6$\frac{1}{2}$ oz.) water-packed tuna (no salt added)
16 pimiento-stuffed olives, chopped (about $\frac{1}{4}$ cup)
2 tablespoons snipped chives
8 slices thinly-sliced rye bread*

Drain the tuna, and flake with a fork.

In a medium-size bowl, whisk the yogurt cheese, horse-radish and Worcestershire sauce until smooth and well blended. Stir in tuna, olives and chives. Use about one-fourth cup of the mixture for each slice of bread. Serve open face.

Makes about 2 cups, for 8 sandwiches.

*Nutritional information page 178.

Per 1/4 cup spread: Calories 65; protein 9 gm; carbohydrates 4 gm; fat 1 gm; cholesterol 8 mg; calcium 112 mg; sodium 296 mg. Exchanges:1/2 lean meat and 1/2 skim milk.

Diet note: To lower sodium, reduce or omit the olives.

Salmon Salad Sandwiches

Stuff tomatoes for a delicious light entree.

$1/2$ cup non-fat yogurt cheese
$1/2$ tablespoon lemon juice
3 tablespoons finely chopped celery
$1/2$ tablespoon finely chopped onion
$1/2$ teaspoon prepared horseradish
$1/4$ teaspoon Worcestershire sauce
1 can ($6^{1}/2$ oz.) pink salmon, drained and flaked
Cucumber slices, optional
9 slices cocktail-size rye or multi-grain bread*

In a medium-size bowl, whisk the yogurt cheese with the lemon juice, celery, onion, horseradish and Worcestershire sauce until smooth. Stir in the salmon.

To serve, spread about 2 tablespoons of mixture on bread and top with cucumber slices.

Makes about $1^{1}/8$ cups, for 9 open-face sandwiches.

*Nutritional information on page 178.

Per 1/4 cup spread (makes 2 sandwiches): Calories 76; protein 10 gm; carbohydrates 2 gm; fat 3 gm; cholesterol 18 mg; calcium 68 mg; sodium 252 mg. Exchanges: 1 lean meat and 1 vegetable.

Diet note: To lower sodium, substitute cooked fresh salmon.

Vegetable Pizza

*Use 3 cups of any vegetables you have on hand. They may be
raw, blanched or cooked, and then chopped, grated or sliced.*

- 1/2 recipe Basic Dough *(recipe, page 140)*
- 2 cups non-fat yogurt cheese
- 1 tablespoon herb seasoning mix
- 3/4 cup sliced mushrooms
- 3/4 cup sliced green onions
- 1/2 cup finely sliced broccoli
- 1/2 cup grated carrot
- 1/2 cup diced yellow bell pepper

Preheat the oven to 450°.

Roll out the dough with a rolling pin, patting into a 10-inch
round. Place on an ungreased pizza pan or cookie sheet, and
prick with a fork. Bake for about 15 minutes until browned. Remove pizza to a rack to cool.

In a medium-size bowl, combine the yogurt cheese and
seasoning; whisk until well blended. Spread on cooled pizza
shell. Arrange vegetables over the top in an attractive pattern.

To serve, cut into 8 wedges.

1 wedge (all-purpose flour): Calories 149; protein 9 gm; carbohydrates 22 gm; fat 3 gm;
cholesterol 0 mg; calcium 226 mg; sodium 178 mg. Exchanges:1 starch/bread, 1 vegetable and 1/2 low fat milk.

1 wedge (flour combination): Calories 148; protein 9 gm; carbohydrates 22 gm; fat 3 gm;
cholesterol 0 mg; calcium 227 mg; sodium 178 mg. Exchanges: 1 starch/bread, 1 vegetable and 1/2 low fat milk.

Turkey Burritos

1/4 cup yogurt cheese
6 tablespoons mild or medium salsa
1 canned green chile (4 tsp.), drained and diced
8 flour tortillas, 6-inch diameter
1 pound turkey breast, thinly sliced
2 cups shredded lettuce, lightly packed

Combine yogurt cheese, salsa and chile in a small bowl and whisk to blend. Spread on one side of each tortilla to within one-fourth inch of edge. Arrange turkey evenly over yogurt cheese; top with lettuce. Roll up the tortillas.
Makes 8 burritos.

Per burrito: Calories 175; protein 20 gm; carbohydrates 15 gm; fat 4 gm; cholesterol 39 mg; calcium 87 mg; sodium 241 mg. Exchanges: 1 starch/bread and 2 lean meat.

New England Lobster Roll

Try this versatile mixture as a salad
or thinned with a little clam juice as a dip.

$1/2$ cup non-fat yogurt cheese
$1/4$ cup snipped chives or chopped green onion tops
  Freshly ground black pepper, to taste
$1/2$ pound cooked lobster, finely chopped
 6 hot dog or hamburger buns*

In a medium-size bowl, whisk together the yogurt cheese, chives, and pepper until well blended. Stir in the lobster and mix well. Use about one-fourth cup of the mixture for each roll.
Makes 6.

*Nutritional information on page 178.

Per 1/4 cup spread: Calories 63; protein 10 gm; carbohydrates 3 gm; fat <1 gm; cholesterol 32 mg; calcium 119 mg; sodium 106 mg. Exchanges: 1 lean meat.

Diet note: Although lobster is higher in cholesterol than most seafoods, its low fat content makes it acceptable for occasional use. To reduce cholesterol, other fresh fish (such as salmon, scallops or snapper) may be substituted; those not on a sodium-restricted diet may substitute artificial lobster meat.

4 • SALADS AND DRESSINGS

Mayonnaise . . . 1000 island . . . ranch . . . blue cheese . . .

If you have had to forego creamy dressings, using yogurt cheese as the base will allow you to enjoy rich-tasting salads again.

Even pasta salads and rice salads are possible. Be sure to add the dressing right before serving so that it stays creamy.

Recipes are arranged by calories (low to high) in either one portion of salad or one-fourth cup of dressing. The dressing-only recipes do not include accompaniments in the analysis; tossed greens or a vegetable salad won't change the values very much, but if you make a chicken or potato salad, be sure to add in the nutritional values for the additional ingredients.

For the times you don't want to follow a recipe, improvising is easy. Simply whisk a cup of non-fat yogurt cheese with one or more of the following:

> *1 tablespoon or less Dijon mustard*
> *1 tablespoon lemon juice + 1 tsp. grated lemon peel*
> *1 tablespoon minced fresh herbs or 1 Tsp. dried herbs*
> *   (basil, parsley, chives, tarragon, rosemary)*
> *1 tablespoon capers, drained and chopped*
> *1 tablespoon tomato paste*
> *Minced garlic to taste*

Salsa

1 cup fresh parsley leaves
1 clove garlic, or to taste
2 medium tomatoes
1 medium onion
1 medium-size green bell pepper
$1/2$ teaspoon salt, optional
$1/8$ teaspoon pepper
$1/8$ teaspoon ground cumin
$1/8$ teaspoon chili powder, or to taste
    Green chile peppers or other hot peppers, optional

Drop parsley and garlic through the feed tube of a food processor (metal blade) or blender with the machine running. Cut tomatoes, onion and green pepper into quarters; add with remaining ingredients and pulse until the desired texture is reached (should be a little chunky).
    Serve with Baked Corn Chips *(recipe, page 138).*

- *Quick Idea.* Mix Salsa with yogurt cheese to make dips and spreads, or heat for a pasta sauce.

Per 2 tablespoons: Calories 5; protein <1 gm; carbohydrates 1 gm; fat tr; cholesterol 0 mg; calcium 5 mg; sodium 2 mg. Exchanges: free food.

Tomato Sauce

⅓ cup water
¼ cup red wine vinegar
1 tablespoon tomato paste
1 tablespoon chopped green onion
1 teaspoon dried tarragon
1 large tomato, peeled, seeded and cut into quarters
2 cups tomato juice (no salt added)
¼ teaspoon black pepper, or to taste
   Salt, optional

Combine water, vinegar, tomato paste, onion and tarragon in a saucepan; simmer over high heat until it has reduced to 1/3 cup.

Cool slightly and pour into food processor or blender. Add tomato and process until smooth. With the machine running add tomato juice. Season to taste.

Makes about 3 cups.

Per 1/2 cup: Calories 27; protein 1 gm; carbohydrates 6 gm; fat <1 gm; cholesterol 0 mg; calcium 13 mg; sodium 7 mg. Exchanges: 1 vegetable.

Horseradish Mousse

Zesty condiment with meat or cold cuts.

1 envelope unflavored gelatin
1/4 cup cold water
2 cups non-fat yogurt cheese
1/3 cup prepared horseradish
Salt and pepper, optional

Sprinkle gelation over cold water in a small bowl. Allow to stand for 10 minutes. Place the bowl in a saucepan containing a small amount of simmering water and stir until dissolved. Cool.

In a medium-size bowl, whisk the yogurt cheese, horseradish and seasonings. Add the gelatin and stir well.

Wet a 7-inch springform pan or 2 1/2 cup mold with cold water and shake out excess water (or oil lightly). Fill with horseradish mixture. Rap the mold on counter gently, then cover and chill at least 4 hours to set.

Unmold onto a bed of lettuce. Cut into 16 pieces.

Per piece: Calories 24; protein 3 gm; carbohydrates 3 gm; fat <1 gm; cholesterol 0 mg; calcium 73 mg; sodium 25 mg. Exchanges: 1 vegetable.

• ***Variation.*** For a dip or sandwich spread, omit the gelatin and water.

Cucumber Mold

2 envelopes unflavored gelatin
1/3 cup cold water
2 large cucumbers, peeled, seeded and finely chopped
2 cups non-fat yogurt cheese
1 small clove garlic, minced
1/2 teaspoon dried dill weed
1/4 teaspoon salt
1/4 cup minced onion
1/4 cup minced fresh parsley
1 head curly endive

Sprinkle gelatin over cold water in a small bowl. Allow to stand for 10 minutes. Place the bowl over simmering water in a saucepan and stir until dissolved. Cool.

Drain the cucumber in a colander and pat dry with towels.

In a large bowl, combine the yogurt cheese, garlic, dill and salt, and whisk until smooth. Stir in the cucumber, onion and parsley. Add gelatin mixture and stir until well blended.

Wet a 1-quart ring mold with cold water and shake out excess water (or lightly oil). Fill with cucumber mixture. Rap the mold on counter gently, then cover and chill at least 6 hours to set. Unmold onto a bed of endive.

Makes about 4 cups.

Per 1/2 cup: Calories 55; protein 7 gm; carbohydrates 6 gm; fat tr; cholesterol 0 mg; calcium 156 mg; sodium 116 mg. Exchanges: 1/2 skim milk.

Thousand Island Dressing

For tossed greens or a fish salad.

1 cup non-fat yogurt cheese
$1/4$ cup ketchup (low-sodium)
1 heaping tablespoon drained dill pickle relish
$1/2$ teaspoon prepared horseradish
$1/4$ teaspoon Dijon-style mustard
    Dash teriyaki sauce
    Salt, optional

Combine all ingredients in a medium-size bowl and whisk until well blended. Cover and chill until serving time.

Use as a salad dressing or as a dip for whole mushrooms, cherry tomatoes and spears of romaine lettuce.

Makes about $1\,1/4$ cups.

Per 1/4 cup dressing: Calories 38; protein 4 gm; carbohydrates 4 gm; fat <1gm; cholesterol 0 mg; calcium 114 mg; sodium 57 mg. Exchanges: 1/2 skim milk.

Caper Dressing

For cold fish or chicken salad.

1 cup non-fat yogurt cheese
1 small clove garlic, minced
$1/2$ teaspoon prepared horseradish
$1/4$ teaspoon Tabasco sauce
2 tablespoons snipped fresh chives
2 tablespoons chopped fresh parsley
$1/2$ tablespoon chopped capers

In a medium-size bowl, whisk yogurt cheese, garlic, horseradish and Tabasco until blended. Add remaining ingredients and mix well. Cover and chill until serving time.

Makes about 1 cup.

Per 1/4 cup dressing: Calories 42; protein 5 gm; carbohydrates 5 gm; fat <1 gm; cholesterol 0 mg; calcium 146 mg; sodium 66 mg. Exchanges: 1/2 skim milk

Calcutta Dressing

Can also be a dip for fresh vegetables
or a sauce for cold fish.

1 cup non-fat yogurt cheese
1 teaspoon very finely minced onion
1 teaspoon prepared horseradish
1 teaspoon tarragon vinegar
1 teaspoon curry powder

    Combine all ingredients in a medium-size bowl and whisk until well blended. Cover and chill until serving time.
    Makes about 1 cup.

Per 1/4 cup dressing: Calories 43; protein 5 gm; carbohydrates 5 gm; fat <1 gm; cholesterol 0 mg; calcium 144 mg; sodium 41 mg. Exchanges: 1/2 skim milk.

• ***Chicken Salad.*** Combine 1 recipe Calcutta Dressing with 2 cups diced cooked chicken and 1/4 pound seedless grapes.

Mustard Dressing

For roast beef, vegetable or potato salad.

1 cup non-fat yogurt cheese
$^1/_2$ heaping tablespoon powdered mustard
1 heaping tablespoon Dijon-style mustard
    Salt, optional

Combine all ingredients in a medium-size bowl and whisk until well blended. Cover and chill until serving time.
Makes about 1 cup.

Per 1/4 cup dressing: Calories 45; protein 5 gm; carbohydrates 5 gm; fat <1 gm; cholesterol 0 mg; calcium 147 mg; sodium 95 mg. Exchanges: 1/2 skim milk.

• **Mayonnaise.** *If you avoid mayonnaise because of the fat and calories, here are two options you will like.*

#1. Whisk 1 cup non-fat yogurt cheese with 1/2 to 1 tablespoon tarragon vinegar or lemon juice (to taste).

#2. Whisk 1 cup non-fat yogurt cheese with 1/4 cup light or no-cholesterol mayonnaise.

Now your friends won't be hearing, "hold the mayo" anymore!

Green Peppercorn Dressing

This dressing is very strong and flavorful, so use more or less mustard and peppercorns, according to your taste.

1 teaspoon water-packed green peppercorns, drained
$1/4$ cup Dijon-style mustard
1 small clove garlic, minced
1 cup non-fat yogurt cheese

In a medium-size bowl, crush the peppercorns with the back of a spoon. Add mustard, garlic and yogurt cheese; mix with a wire whisk until well blended. Cover and chill until serving time.

Makes about $1^1/4$ cups.

Per 1/4 cup dressing (not including peppercorns, for which no information is available): Calories 45; protein 4 gm; carbohydrates 4 gm; fat 1 gm; cholesterol 0 mg; calcium 128 mg; sodium 189 mg. Exchanges: 1/2 skim milk.

Diet note: To reduce sodium, use less mustard.

• ***Chicken and Potato Salad.*** Combine 1 recipe Green Peppercorn Dressing with 2 cups diced cooked chicken and 1 cup diced cooked potato.

Potato Salad

For an attractive salad, toss with cooked green beans.

2 pounds small red new potatoes, scrubbed
1 cup non-fat yogurt cheese
¹/₄ cup light mayonnaise
¹/₄ cup chopped onion or green onion
1 teaspoon dill weed
   Salt and pepper, optional
   Dill sprigs, optional garnish

Place potatoes in boiling water to cover, and simmer until tender, 12 to 15 minutes. Drain and cool.

Place yogurt cheese, mayonnaise, onion and seasonings in a large bowl and whisk well to combine. Quarter the potatoes and add; toss lightly but well. Chill several hours.

Makes 7 cups.

Per 1/2 cup salad: Calories 77; protein 3 gm; carbohydrates 15 gm; fat 1 gm; cholesterol 1 mg; calcium 45 mg; sodium 37 mg. Exchanges: 1 starch/bread.

- ***Sweet Potato Salad.*** For a new taste, use peeled sweet potatoes, and substitute vinegar for the dill weed.

Dijon Dressing

*Can also be served as a fondue for dipping cooked
meat cubes, or as a sandwich spread.*

 $^3/_4$ cup non-fat yogurt cheese
 4 teaspoons coarsely ground Dijon-style mustard
 1 clove garlic, minced
 1 tablespoon minced onion
 2 teaspoons tarragon vinegar
 $^1/_2$ tablespoon minced fresh parsley
 Pinch *each* dried basil and dried marjoram

Combine all ingredients in a medium-size bowl and whisk until smooth. Cover and chill until serving time.

Makes about $^3/_4$ cup.

Per 1/4 cup dressing: Calories 50; protein 5 gm; carbohydrates 5 gm; fat 1 gm; cholesterol 0 mg; calcium 155 mg; sodium 128 mg. Exchanges: 1/2 skim milk.

• ***Beef and Potato Salad.*** Combine 1 recipe Dijon Dressing with 2 cups leftover cooked lean beef or steak and 2 cooked, medium-size potatoes.

Neapolitan Dressing

For a seafood salad.

1 cup non-fat yogurt cheese
2 tablespoons chili sauce
2 tablespoons grated Parmesan cheese
1 teaspoon prepared horseradish
$^1/_2$ teaspoon dried oregano

Combine all ingredients in a medium-size bowl and whisk until smooth. Cover and chill until serving time.
Makes about 1 cup.

Per 1/4 cup dressing: Calories 54; protein 6 gm; carbohydrates 5 gm; fat 1 gm; cholesterol 2 mg; calcium 79 mg; sodium 88 mg. Exchanges: 1 lowfat milk.

Shrimp Mold

An inexpensive way to serve a favorite.

$^1/_4$ cup cold water
1 envelope unflavored gelatin
1 can (6$^1/_2$ oz.) shrimp
1$^3/_4$ cups non-fat yogurt cheese
$^1/_2$ cup ketchup (low-sodium)
$^1/_2$ cup *each* minced celery and minced onion

Sprinkle gelatin over cold water in a small bowl. Allow to stand for 10 minutes. Place the bowl in a saucepan containing a small amount of simmering water and stir until dissolved. Cool.

Drain the shrimp. Immerse in ice water for 5 minutes, then drain again.

In a medium-size bowl, whisk yogurt cheese and ketchup until smooth. Gently stir in shrimp, celery, onion and dissolved gelatin. Mix well.

Wet a 3-cup mold with cold water and shake out the excess water (or lightly oil). Fill with shrimp mixture. Rap the mold on the counter gently, then cover and chill 3 to 4 hours to set.

To serve, unmold onto a platter and surround with melba toast rounds.

Makes about 3 cups.

Per 1/2 cup: Calories 101; protein 14 gm; carbohydrates 8 gm; fat 1 gm; cholesterol 46 mg; calcium 205 mg; sodium 107 mg. Exchanges: 1 lean meat and1/2 skim milk.

Diet note: Although shrimp is higher in cholesterol than most seafoods, its low fat content makes it acceptable for occasional use. To lower cholesterol, other fresh fish (such as salmon, scallops or snapper) may be substituted; those not on a sodium-restricted diet may substitute artificial lobster meat.

Caribbean Crab Mold

This is very peppery; you may want to use less black pepper.

    1 envelope unflavored gelatin
  ¼ cup cold water
1¾ cups non-fat yogurt cheese
    2 tablespoons dry sherry
  ½ teaspoon seasoned salt (or herb seasoning)
  ¼ teaspoon *each* ground black and red pepper (cayenne)
    1 jar (2 oz.) diced pimientos, well drained
    6 ounces cooked crab meat, flaked
       Fresh parsley sprigs and mango slices, optional garnish

Sprinkle gelatin over cold water in a small bowl. Allow to stand for 10 minutes. Place the bowl in a saucepan containing a small amount of simmering water and stir until dissolved. Cool.

In a medium-size bowl, whisk the yogurt cheese, sherry and seasonings until smooth. Add the gelatin and pimientos and mix well. Gently fold in the crab.

Wet a 3-cup ring mold with cold water and shake out excess water (or lightly oil). Fill with crab mixture. Rap the mold on counter gently, then cover and chill at least 5 hours to set.

To serve, unmold onto a platter; garnish with parsley sprigs and mango slices, if desired. Serve with crackers.

Makes about 2½ cups.

Per 1/4 cup: Calories 52; protein 7 gm; carbohydrates 4 gm; fat <1 gm; cholesterol 17 mg; calcium 106 mg; sodium 130 mg. Exchanges: 1/2 skim milk.

Diet note: Although crab is higher in cholesterol than most seafoods, its low fat content makes it acceptable for occasional use. To reduce cholesterol, other fresh fish (such as salmon, scallops or snapper) may be substituted; those not on a sodium-restricted diet may substitute artificial crab meat.

Salmon Mousse

1 envelope unflavored gelatin
2 teaspoons lemon juice
$^1/_2$ cup water
1 medium onion, quartered
1 can (7$^3/_4$ oz.) pink salmon, drained
1$^1/_2$ cups yogurt cheese
1 heaping teaspoon dried dill weed
$^1/_2$ teaspoon paprika

Sprinkle the gelatin over lemon juice and water in a small bowl. Allow to stand for 10 minutes. Place the bowl in a saucepan containing a small amount of simmering water, and stir until dissolved. Cool slightly.

Chop onion in a food processor or blender. Add remaining ingredients, including gelatin, and process until almost smooth. Transfer to a 2$^1/_2$ cup mold and chill at least 4 hours.

To serve, unmold onto lettuce leaves.

Makes about 2$^1/_4$ cups.

• *Note:* Canned salmon bones mash easily, and add calcium. The nutritional analysis below includes the bones.

Per 1/2 cup (includes salmon bones): Calories 136; protein 18 gm; carbohydrates 7 gm; fat 4 gm; cholesterol 17 mg; calcium 292 mg; sodium 245 mg. Exchanges: 2 lean meat and 1/2 skim milk.

Diet note: To reduce sodium, substitute cooked fresh salmon, bones removed.

Pecan Parsley Dressing

1 cup cucumber (1 lg.) peeled, seeded and minced
2 cups non-fat yogurt cheese
1 clove garlic, minced
$1/2$ teaspoon paprika
   Salt, optional
   Dash ground red pepper (cayenne)
$3/4$ cup finely chopped pecans
$1/2$ cup fresh parsley leaves, finely chopped

Drain the cucumber in a colander for 20 to 30 minutes. Pat dry with a towel.

In a medium-size bowl, combine the yogurt cheese, garlic, paprika, salt and pepper; whisk until smooth. Stir in cucumber, pecans and parsley and mix well. Cover and chill until serving time.

Makes about $2^{1}/_{2}$ cups.

Per 1/4 cup dressing: Calories 89; protein 4 gm; carbohydrates 6 gm; fat 6 gm; cholesterol 0 mg; calcium 121 mg; sodium 34 mg. Exchanges: 1/2 skim milk and 1 fat.

Diet note: To reduce fat and calories, reduce or eliminate the nuts.

- **Turkey Salad.** Add 3 to 4 cups diced cooked turkey to 1 recipe Pecan Parsley Dressing.

Vegetable Terrine

This tasty appetizer looks like it takes ages to make, but it doesn't.

 2 thin carrots (less than 1" diameter)
 6 mushrooms
 2 thin zucchini, cut in half lengthwise
12 green beans
$1/2$ red bell pepper, seeded and cut in strips
$1/2$ cup cooked green peas
 2 envelopes unflavored gelatin
$1/3$ cup cold water
$3^1/2$ cups non-fat yogurt cheese
 2 large cloves garlic, minced
 3 tablespoons finely chopped fresh basil, oregano
    or tarragon, or a mixture
 1 tablespoon minced fresh parsley
    Salt and pepper, optional
    Tabasco sauce to taste
    Tomato Sauce *(recipe, page 91)*

In a large pot of boiling water, blanch each vegetable separately until just tender.* Remove and plunge into cold water to stop the cooking. Drain well and pat dry with towels.

Sprinkle the gelatin over cold water in a small bowl. Allow to stand for 10 minutes. Place bowl in a saucepan containing a small amount of simmering water and stir until dissolved. Cool.

Whisk yogurt cheese, garlic, herbs, parsley and seasonings until smooth. Add the gelatin and whisk until well blended.

Line an 8 x 4 loaf pan with plastic wrap. Place the pan with the long (8-inch) side facing you. Spread one-third of the yogurt cheese mixture on the bottom.

Starting about 1/2 inch from the long side closest to you, arrange a row of carrots end-to-end.

Leave about a 1/2-inch space, and then arrange a row of mushrooms, caps facing down, stems up.

Leave another 1/2-inch space, and then arrange a row of zucchini.

There should be a 1/4-inch space between the zucchini and the other long side of the pan. (The uneven spacing will give each slice a checkerboard pattern of shapes, colors and textures, when cut.)

Press the vegetables down gently, and spread with half the remaining yogurt cheese mixture.

Now, starting about 1/4 inch from the long side closest to you, arrange a row of peas.

Leave about a 1/2-inch space, and then arrange a row of red pepper strips, end-to-end.

Leave a 1/2-inch space, and then arrange a row of green beans end-to-end.

Press the vegetables down gently, and top with remaining yogurt cheese mixture.

Cover and chill at least 6 hours.

Unmold and cut into 8 slices. Serve with tomato sauce *(recipe, page 91).*

Serves 8.

*Other vegetables can be used, such as 1 tomato, peeled, seeded, cut into strips; 1/4 pound cooked spinach, chopped and squeezed dry; 4 ounces broccoli flowerets. Or any leftover vegetables you have on hand.

Per slice (not including sauce): Calories 112; protein 11 gm; carbohydrates 15 gm; fat 1 gm; cholesterol 0 mg; calcium 290 mg; sodium 82 mg. Exchanges: 1 vegetable and 1 skim milk.

Mock Chicken Salad

It's hard to believe there is no chicken in this salad.

2   cups non-fat yogurt cheese
1   teaspoon seasoned salt (or herb seasoning)
1   can (6$^1/_2$ oz.) crushed pineapple (packed in own juice)
1   cup chopped pecans
$^1/_2$ cup chopped red or green bell pepper, or mixed
$^1/_4$ cup finely minced onion

   In a medium-size bowl, whisk yogurt cheese and seasoned salt until smooth and well blended. Drain the pineapple and stir into yogurt cheese mixture with remaining ingredients. Cover and chill until serving time.
   Makes about 2$^3/_4$ cups.

Per 1/4 cup: Calories 106; protein 4 gm; carbohydrates 8 gm; fat 7 gm; cholesterol 0 mg; calcium 109 mg; sodium 148 mg. Exchanges: 1/2 skim milk and 1 fat.

Diet note: To lower fat and calories, reduce the nuts.

- -
Variation: Add some diced chicken or turkey.
- -

Blue Cheese Mold

2 teaspoons unflavored gelatin
$\frac{1}{4}$ cup cold water
$2\frac{1}{2}$ cups non-fat yogurt cheese
$\frac{1}{8}$ teaspoon ground red pepper (cayenne)
1 pound blue cheese, crumbled
$\frac{1}{4}$ cup snipped chives or green onion tops
    Paprika, garnish

Sprinkle gelatin over cold water in a small bowl. Allow to stand for 10 minutes. Place the bowl in a saucepan containing a small amount of simmering water and stir until dissolved. Cool.

In a large bowl, whisk the yogurt cheese and pepper until smooth. Blend in blue cheese and chives. Add gelatin and stir well. Wet a 1-quart mold with cold water and shake out excess water (or lightly oil). Fill with cheese mixture. Rap the mold on counter gently, then cover and chill at least 5 hours to set.

Unmold onto a platter and sprinkle with paprika. Serve with crackers, apples, pears and grapes.

Makes about $3\frac{3}{4}$ cups.

Per 1/4 cup: Calories 134; protein 10 gm; carbohydrates 4 gm; fat 9 gm; cholesterol 22 mg; calcium 254 mg; sodium 449 mg. Exchanges: 1 high fat meat and 1/2 skim milk.

Diet note: Although blue cheese is high in fat, cholesterol and sodium, combining it with yogurt cheese gives full flavor while lowering these values. Not recommended for those on low-sodium diets.

• **Variation.** For a blue cheese spread, omit gelatin and water.

Mandarin Orange Salad

For a less chunky texture, cut up the orange segments.

1 cup non-fat yogurt cheese
1 tablespoon honey (orange blossom, if available)
¹/₂ teaspon vanilla extract
¹/₄ teaspoon ground cardamom
1 can (11 oz.) mandarin orange segments, well drained

In a medium-size bowl, combine the yogurt cheese with honey, vanilla and cardamom and whisk until smooth. Add the orange segments and mix gently.

To serve, spoon into 2 bowls.

Per serving: Calories 169; protein 10 gm; carbohydrates 31 gm; fat <1 gm; cholesterol 0 mg; calcium 298 mg; sodium 89 mg. Exchanges: 1 fruit and 1 skim milk.

Chutney Chicken Salad

The taste of India!

1 cup non-fat yogurt cheese
1 jar (8 oz.) Major Grey's chutney
1 teaspoon curry powder, optional
  Salt and pepper, optional
2 cups chopped cooked turkey or chicken breast
3 cups chopped celery
$1/3$ cup chopped walnuts

Combine yogurt cheese, chutney, curry, salt and pepper in a large bowl and whisk until smooth and well blended. Blend in the remaining ingredients and mix lightly to coat with the yogurt cheese mixture. Cover and chill until serving time.

Makes about $4^1/2$ cups.

Per 1/2 cup: Calories 154; protein 13 gm; carbohydrates 14 gm; fat 4 gm; cholesterol 22 mg; calcium 40 mg; sodium 107 mg. Exchanges: 1 lean meat, 1 vegetable and 1/2 low fat milk.

Diet note: To lower fat and calories, reduce or eliminate the nuts and chutney.

5 · CHILLED SOUPS

All of these soups are served chilled, but some require cooking and some do not. They all taste like they've been enriched with cream, so you may have difficulty believing that they are truly low in fat and calories.

Again, the recipes are arranged according to calories, from lowest to highest. Although the nutritional analysis was calculated for one cup of soup, this is a larger portion than you are likely to want for snacking or even as a mealtime serving. One-half to three-fourths of a cup is probably closer to what you will use. Most of the soups thicken as they stand, and will need to have water added before serving. This, of course, will reduce the calories!

Surprisingly, most of these soups also make great dips or spreads.

Celery Bisque

5 cups chicken broth or stock (low-sodium)
3 cups chopped celery, including leaves
1 cup chopped green onion, including some green tops
1 cup non-fat yogurt cheese
   Salt and pepper, optional
   Snipped chives or sliced green onion tops, garnish

Combine chicken broth, celery and green onions in a large saucepan. Bring to a boil, then lower heat and simmer, covered, for about 15 minutes. Allow to cool.

In a large bowl, whisk the yogurt cheese until smooth.

Working in batches, puree soup in a food processor (metal blade) or blender, and whisk gradually into the yogurt cheese. Season to taste. Cover and chill for about 4 hours.

Just before serving, add a little water if soup has thickened, and adjust the seasonings. Garnish each bowl with a sprinkle of chives.

Makes about 6 cups.

Per cup: Calories 66; protein 6 gm; carbohydrates 8 gm; fat 1 gm; cholesterol 0 mg; calcium 126 mg; sodium 144 mg. Exchanges: 1 vegetable and 1/2 skim milk.

Cucumber Soup

No cooking!

3 medium cucumbers, peeled and seeded
2 green onions
1 cup non-fat yogurt cheese
1 tablespoon snipped dill, or 1 teaspoon dried dill weed
1 tablespoon Worcestershire sauce
1 tablespoon lemon juice
$1/4$ teaspoon celery seed
$1/2$ teaspoon salt
    Black pepper to taste

Finely chop cucumbers and green onions. Combine with remaining ingredients and puree in blender until smooth (or place all the ingredients in a food processor and process until smooth). Cover and chill about 3 hours.

At serving time, add a little water if mixture has thickened, and adjust seasonings.

Makes about 3 cups.

Per cup: Calories 73; protein 7 gm; carbohydrates 10 gm; fat <1 gm; cholesterol 0 mg; calcium 217 mg; sodium 474 mg. Exchanges: 1 vegetable and 1/2 skim milk.

Diet note: Omitting salt will lower sodium to 73 mg. Herb seasoning may be substituted.

Mushroom Bisque

1   pound sliced mushrooms
4   cups chicken broth or stock (low-sodium)
1/4   cup dry sherry
1   cup non-fat yogurt cheese
1/4   teaspoon salt
    Pepper to taste

In a large saucepan, cook the mushrooms over low heat for about 15 minutes. Add the chicken broth. Bring to a boil, then reduce heat and simmer, covered, for 10 minutes.

With a slotted spoon, remove mushrooms to a food processor (metal blade) or blender. Add the sherry and process until smooth. Return to the saucepan and stir. Allow to cool.

In a large bowl, whisk the yogurt cheese, salt and pepper until smooth. Gradually whisk in mushroom mixture. Cover and chill about 4 hours.

Just before serving, add a little water if soup has thickened, and adjust seasonings.

Makes about 6 cups.

Per cup: Calories 80; protein 6 gm; carbohydrates 9 gm; fat 1 gm; cholesterol 0 mg; calcium 99 mg; sodium 172 mg. Exchanges: 1 vegetable and 1/2 skim milk.

Diet note: To reduce sodium, omit the salt.

Curried Eggplant Soup

An unusually delicious cold soup.

1   medium eggplant (about 1¼ lbs.)
½ cup chopped onion
1   tablespoon curry powder
4   cups chicken broth or stock (low-sodium)
¾ cup non-fat yogurt cheese
    Salt and white pepper, optional
    Minced fresh parsley, garnish

Trim and peel eggplant, and cut into ½-inch cubes. Combine with onion and curry powder in a large saucepan. Add the chicken broth. Bring to a boil, then lower heat, cover and simmer about 30 minutes or until the eggplant is very soft. Remove from heat and allow to cool.

In a large bowl, whisk the yogurt cheese until smooth.

Working in batches, puree the eggplant mixture in a food processor (metal blade) or blender. Strain through a fine sieve, and whisk into the yogurt cheese; season to taste. Cover and chill for about 4 hours.

Just before serving, add a little water if the soup has thickened, and adjust seasonings. Garnish each bowl with minced parsley.

Makes about 5 cups.

Per cup: Calories 87; protein 6 gm; carbohydrates 13 gm; fat 2 gm; cholesterol 0 mg; calcium 135 mg; sodium 89 mg. Exchanges: 1 vegetable and 1/2 lowfat milk.

Creamy Gazpacho

No cooking!

1 cup non-fat yogurt cheese
1 clove garlic, minced
   Dash Tabasco sauce
3 cups tomato juice (low-sodium)
1 large cucumber, peeled, seeded and chopped finely
1 medium onion, chopped finely
1 green bell pepper, diced
   Chopped fresh parsley, garnish

Combine the yogurt cheese, garlic and Tabasco in a large bowl and whisk until smooth. Blend in the tomato juice. Stir in cucumber, onion and green pepper. Cover and chill about 3 hours.

At serving time, add a little water if mixture has thickened, and adjust seasonings. Sprinkle with chopped parsley.

Makes about 4$\frac{1}{4}$ cups.

Per cup: Calories 87; protein 6 gm; carbohydrates 15 gm; fat tr; cholesterol 0 mg; calcium 156 mg; sodium 46 mg. Exchanges: 2 vegetables and 1/2 skim milk.

Tomato Soup

No cooking!

1 cup non-fat yogurt cheese
1 tablespoon finely minced onion
1 tablespoon finely minced celery
2 cups tomato juice (low-sodium)
   Dash Tabasco sauce
   Salt and pepper, optional
   Thin lemon slices, optional garnish

Combine yogurt cheese, onion and celery in a large bowl and whisk until well blended. Gradually stir in tomato juice and mix well. Season to taste with Tabasco, salt and pepper (or try an extra-spicy herb blend). Cover and chill about 3 hours.

At serving time, add a little water if mixture has thickened, and adjust the seasonings. Garnish each serving with a slice of lemon.

Makes about $2^3/_4$ cups.

Per cup: Calories 94; protein 8 gm; carbohydrates 14 gm; fat <1 gm; cholesterol 0 mg; calcium 219 mg; sodium 68 mg. Exchanges: 2 vegetables and 1/2 skim milk.

• ***Creamy Bloody Mary (variation):*** Add vodka; serve in mugs.

Asparagus Soup

2¹/₂ cups chicken broth or stock (low-sodium)
3 cups fresh asparagus, cut into pieces
¹/₂ cup peeled, diced potatoes
¹/₄ cup chopped onion
1 cup non-fat yogurt cheese
1 teaspoon curry powder
¹/₄ teaspoon salt, or to taste
Pinch black pepper

Combine chicken broth, asparagus, potatoes and onion in a medium-size saucepan. Bring to a boil, then reduce heat and simmer, covered, until potato is cooked, about 15 minutes. Allow to cool.

In a large bowl, combine the yogurt cheese, curry powder, salt and pepper.

Working in batches, puree the asparagus mixture in a food processor (metal blade), and whisk gradually into the yogurt cheese mixture. Cover and chill about 3 hours.

Just before serving, add a little water if the soup has thickened, and adjust seasonings.

Makes about 4 cups.

Per cup: Calories 104; protein 10 gm; carbohydrates 14 gm; fat 1 gm; cholesterol 0 mg; calcium 168 mg; sodium 228 mg. Exchanges: 1 vegetable and 1 skim milk.

Diet note: Omitting salt will lower sodium to 90 mg.

Curried Pea Soup

2½ cups chicken broth or stock (low-sodium)
1 package (10 oz.) frozen green peas
1 small onion, chopped
1 clove garlic, minced
2 teaspoons curry powder, or more to taste
½ teaspoon dry mustard
   Salt and pepper, optional
1 cup non-fat yogurt cheese
   Major Grey's chutney, optional garnish

Combine chicken broth, peas, onion, garlic, curry powder, dry mustard, salt and pepper in a large saucepan. Bring to a boil, then reduce heat, cover and simmer for about 15 minutes. Allow to cool.

In a large bowl, whisk the yogurt cheese until smooth.

Working in batches if necessary, puree the soup mixture in a food processor (metal blade) or blender. Strain through a fine sieve, and whisk into the yogurt cheese. Thin to desired consistency with a little chicken broth or water. Cover and chill for about 4 hours.

Just before serving, add a little water if soup has thickened, and adjust seasonings. Garnish each bowl with a dollop of chutney, if desired.

Makes about 5 cups.

Per cup: Calories 105; protein 8 gm; carbohydrates 15 gm; fat 1 gm; cholesterol 0 mg; calcium 138 mg; sodium 124 mg. Exchanges: 2 vegetables and 1/2 skim milk.

Cauliflower Soup

 1 large head cauliflower, trimmed and broken into flowerets
 1 large onion, coarsely chopped
 3 tablespoons light margarine
 1/4 cup all-purpose flour
 1 quart buttermilk
 1 cup non-fat yogurt cheese
 2 tablespoons prepared horseradish
    Salt and pepper, optional
    Tabasco sauce to taste
    Chopped fresh parsley or dill, garnish

In a large saucepan, saute cauliflower and onion in melted margarine, tossing gently, for about 5 minutes. Remove from heat and sprinkle with flour. Stir in buttermilk and return to heat. Bring to a boil; reduce heat, cover and simmer until cauliflower is very soft, about 25 minutes. Allow to cool. (Mixture may look curdled.)

In a large bowl, whisk yogurt cheese, horseradish and seasonings until smooth.

Working in batches, process cauliflower mixture in a food processor (metal blade) or blender until the texture is coarse (like grits). Gradually whisk into the yogurt cheese. Taste and adjust seasonings to give a bit of a tang. Cover and chill for about 4 hours.

Just before serving, add a little water if the soup has thickened, and adjust seasonings; add garnish.

Makes 8 cups.

Per cup: Calories 123; protein 8 gm; carbohydrates 15 gm; fat 3 gm; cholesterol 5 mg; calcium 237 mg; sodium 213 mg. Exchanges: 1/2 lowfat milk.

Diet note: Reduce sodium by using low-sodium buttermilk.

Creamy Taco Soup

1 medium onion, chopped
1 clove garlic, minced
1 tablespoon corn oil
2 cups non-fat yogurt cheese
$\frac{1}{2}$ teaspoon ground cumin
1 cup chicken broth or stock (low-sodium)
$\frac{3}{4}$ cup medium-hot picante salsa
   Grated sharp Cheddar cheese, optional garnish
   Sliced black olives, optional garnish

Saute onion and garlic in oil until soft. Remove from heat.

In a large bowl, whisk the yogurt cheese and cumin until smooth. Add the broth slowly, along with the salsa, onion and garlic, beating until well blended. Cover and chill about 3 hours.

Just before serving, add a little water if the soup has thickened, and adjust seasonings. Garnish each bowl with grated Cheddar cheese and sliced black olives, if desired.

Makes about 4 cups.

Per cup: Calories 127; protein 11 gm; carbohydrates 12 gm; fat 4 gm; cholesterol 0 mg; calcium 289 mg; sodium 298 mg. Exchanges: 1 skim milk and 1 fat.

Diet note: To lower fat and calories, microwave the onion and garlic, eliminating the oil. To lower sodium, use homemade salsa *(recipe, page 90).*

• *Variation.* For a dip, omit the chicken stock. Scoop up with corn chips *(recipe, page 138),* fill taco shells (add shredded lettuce and salsa), or top a baked potato.

Shrimp Soup

No cooking!

1 can (28 oz.) Italian plum tomatoes
1 clove garlic, minced
3 cups non-fat yogurt cheese
4 green onions, finely chopped
½ large green bell pepper, chopped
2 tablespoons minced green olives (8 small)
2 tablespoons chopped fresh parsley
1 tablespoon snipped chives
½ pound fresh shrimp, cooked and coarsely chopped
6 ounces flaked crab meat, optional
   Salt and pepper, optional

In a food processor (metal blade) or blender, combine tomatoes and garlic, and process until smooth.

Whisk yogurt cheese in a large bowl until smooth. Gradually whisk in pureed tomatoes. Add remaining ingredients and stir until well blended. Cover and chill about 4 hours.

At serving time, add a little water if mixture has thickened, and adjust seasonings.

Makes about 7 cups.

Per cup: Calories 132; protein 15 gm; carbohydrates 14 gm; fat 2 gm; cholesterol 45 mg; calcium 300 mg; sodium 377 mg. Exchanges: 1 lean meat, 1 vegetable and 1/2 skim milk.

Diet Note: Although shrimp is higher in cholesterol than most seafoods, its low fat content makes it acceptable for occasional use. To lower cholesterol, other fresh fish (such as salmon, scallops or snapper) may be substituted; those not on a sodium-restricted diet may substitute artificial lobster meat. To lower sodium, use 1 1/2 pounds very ripe plum tomatoes (peeled) and reduce or eliminate olives.

Bulgarian Soup

No cooking!

- ¹/₂ cup raisins
- 3 cups non-fat yogurt cheese
- 1 cup peeled, seeded and chopped cucumber
- ³/₄ cup chopped walnuts
- ¹/₄ cup chopped green onion
- ¹/₄ teaspoon salt, or to taste
- Ground black pepper to taste
- Minced fresh parsley and snipped dill, garnish

Soak raisins in water to cover for 15 minutes; drain.

Combine raisins with remaining ingredients and whisk until well blended. Thin with water to desired consistency. Cover and chill about 3 hours.

Just before serving, thin to desired consistency and adjust seasonings. Garnish with parsley and dill.

Makes 4³/₄ cups.

Per cup: Calories 295; protein 16 gm; carbohydrates 30 gm; fat 13 gm; cholesterol 0 mg; calcium 409 mg; sodium 234 mg. Exchanges: 1 starch/bread, 1 lowfat milk and 2 fat.

Diet note: The water you add will automatically lessen all the nutritional values. To further lower calories and fat, omit or reduce walnuts. To lower sodium, eliminate salt.

• **Variation.** For a spread, drain cucumber well, and simply make the soup a day or so ahead. It will become very thick.

6 · FROSTINGS, FILLINGS, FONDUES, SPREADS AND TOPPINGS

The diet you're on does not have to cut down your enjoyment of waffles or pancakes. It doesn't have to mean the end of creamy frostings. Nor does it have to mean *your* dessert fruit must be eaten plain while everyone else is dolloping on whipped cream.

For toast, muffins, rice cakes, graham crackers, and bagels, even crepes and cake, you can still enjoy toppings, fillings and spreads while limiting your intake of fat, cholesterol and calories. Most of the recipes in this chapter are interchangeable for these purposes.

For pancakes, waffles and French toast, I think you will find the sweet spreads are a refreshing change from jam and syrup. Some can even be eaten alone as a snack.

The nutritional information has been based on one-fourth cup (4 tablespoons) of the mixture. In most instances, 2 tablespoons will be adequate. As in other chapters, the recipes are arranged by calories, from lowest to highest.

For a simple, quick and satisfying sweet spread or topping, simply whisk a cup of non-fat yogurt cheese with one or more of the following:

$^1/_2$ *teaspoon ground cinnamon, nutmeg, ginger or cloves*
$^1/_2$ *teaspoon pumpkin pie spice*
1 *tablespoon honey*

2 tablespoons maple syrup

1 teaspoon vanilla extract

¹/₄ teaspoon lemon, orange, cherry or coconut extract

¹/₄ teaspoon peppermint, maple, rum or almond extract

1 teaspoon grated citrus peel

1 tablespoon liqueur

¹/₄ cup finely chopped dried fruit

1 tablespoon unsweetened cocoa powder + a sweetener

Cranberry-Maple Cheese

Low in fat and high in taste.

 $^1/_2$ cup non-fat yogurt cheese
 2 tablespoons maple syrup
 $^1/_8$ teaspoon ground cinnamon
 1 cup fresh cranberries, finely chopped

In a small bowl, whisk the yogurt cheese with the maple syrup and cinnamon until smooth and well blended. Stir in the chopped cranberries. Cover and chill until serving time.

Makes about 1 $^1/_4$ cups.

Per 1/4 cup: Calories 45; protein 2 gm; carbohydrates 9 gm; fat tr; cholesterol 0 mg; calcium 66 mg; sodium 17 mg. Exchanges: 1/2 skim milk.

• *Easy Vanilla Topping.* Use a dollop of yogurt cheese made with vanilla yogurt . . . and nothing else! Kids love it on graham crackers.

Strawberry Dip

Delicious with a platter of fresh fruit.

1   cup non-fat yogurt cheese
1/4 cup natural strawberry preserves, unsweetened
1   tablespoon lemon juice
1   teaspoon grated lemon peel

Combine all ingredients in a medium-size bowl and whisk until well blended and smooth. Cover and chill until serving time. Makes about 1 1/4 cups.

Per 1/4 cup: Calories 48; protein 4 gm; carbohydrates 8 gm; fat <1 gm; cholesterol 0 mg; calcium 115 mg; sodium 49 mg. Exchanges: 1/2 skim milk.

Ginger Lime Dip

Refreshing!

1   cup non-fat yogurt cheese
1   tablespoon *each* lime juice and honey
2   teaspoons grated lime peel
1/2 teaspoon ground ginger

Combine all the ingredients in a medium-size bowl, and whisk until well blended and smooth. Cover and chill until serving time. Makes about 1 cup.

Per 1/4 cup: Calories 58; protein 5 gm; carbohydrates 9 gm; fat tr; cholesterol 0 mg; calcium 143 mg; sodium 41 mg. Exchanges: 1/2 skim milk.

Banana Fondue

Also makes a nice fruit salad dressing.

1 ripe banana, cut into pieces
$^{1}/_{2}$ cup non-fat yogurt cheese
1 tablespoon frozen orange juice concentrate, thawed
$^{1}/_{8}$ teaspoon cinnamon

Combine all ingredients in a food processor (metal blade) or blender and process until smooth. Cover and chill for 1 hour. Serve with fresh fruit chunks or angel food cake cubes. Makes about 1 cup.

Per 1/4 cup: Calories 62; protein 3 gm; carbohydrates 13 gm; fat <1 gm; cholesterol 0 mg; calcium 75 mg; sodium 20 mg. Exchanges: 1 fruit.

Apple-Honey Spread

1 cup non-fat yogurt cheese
2 tablespoons frozen apple juice concentrate, thawed
2 teaspoons honey

Combine all ingredients in a medium-size bowl and whisk until well blended and smooth. Cover and chill until serving time. Makes about 1 cup.

Per 1/4 cup: Calories 66; protein 5 gm; carbohydrates 11 gm; fat <1 gm; cholesterol 0 mg; calcium 142 mg; sodium 41 mg. Exchanges: 1/2 fruit and 1/2 skim milk.

Apricot-Almond Spread

2 tablespoons blanched almonds, toasted lightly and cooled
2 ounces (about $1/3$ cup) dried apricots
$3/4$ cup non-fat yogurt cheese
1 tablespoon honey, or to taste
$1/4$ teaspoon grated lemon peel

In a food processor (metal blade), process the almonds until finely chopped. Add the apricots and process until very finely chopped. Add the remaining ingredients and process until almost smooth. Cover and chill until serving time.

Makes about 1 cup.

Per 1/4 cup: Calories 97; protein 5 gm; carbohydrates 15 gm; fat 2 gm; cholesterol 0 mg; calcium 123 mg; sodium 32 mg. Exchanges: 1 fruit and 1 fat.

Fruit Fondue

Rich-tasting!

1/2 cup non-fat yogurt cheese
2 tablespoons light brown sugar
3/4 teaspoon grated orange peel

Combine all ingredients in a small bowl and whisk until smooth and well blended. Cover and chill until serving time.
Makes about 1/2 cup.

Per 1/4 cup: Calories 92; protein 5 gm; carbohydrates 18 gm; fat <1; cholesterol 0 mg; calcium 153 mg; sodium 44 mg. Exchanges: 1 fruit and 1/2 skim milk.

• ***Easy Lemon Topping.*** Use a dollop of yogurt cheese made with lemon yogurt . . . and nothing else! Lemon-lovers' paradise!

Tangy Florida Orange Spread

Without the liqueur, this is a good after-school snack.

1 cup non-fat yogurt cheese
1/4 cup light brown sugar or confectioners' sugar
1 tablespoon frozen orange juice concentrate, thawed
1 tablespoon grated orange peel
1 tablespoon orange liqueur, optional

Combine all ingredients in a medium-size bowl and whisk until smooth. Cover and chill until serving time. Makes about 1 cup.

Per 1/4 cup: Calories 99; protein 5 gm; carbohydrates 20 gm; fat tr; cholesterol 0 mg; calcium 155 mg; sodium 44 mg. Exchanges: 1 fruit and 1/2 skim milk.

• ***Easy Lo-Cal Peanut Butter Spread.*** To satisfy a peanut butter craving, combine 1 tablespoon peanut butter with 3 or 4 tablespoons non-fat yogurt cheese.

Hawaiian Cream

A sweet-tangy taste of the Pacific.

1 cup non-fat yogurt cheese
1 teaspoon grated fresh gingerroot
$\frac{1}{2}$ cup finely chopped walnuts, pecans or macadamia nuts
$\frac{1}{3}$ cup well-drained crushed pineapple, packed in own juice

    In a medium-size bowl, whisk yogurt cheese and ginger until smooth. Blend in the nuts and pineapple. Cover and chill until serving time.
    Makes about 1$\frac{1}{2}$ cups.

Per 1/4 cup: Calories 99; protein 5 gm; carbohydrates 7 gm; fat 6 gm; cholesterol 0 mg; calcium 105 mg; sodium 28 mg. Exchanges: 1/2 skim milk and 1 fat.

Diet note: To reduce fat and calories, reduce or eliminate the nuts.

Date-Nut Spread

1 cup non-fat yogurt cheese
2 teaspoons grated orange peel
$\frac{1}{2}$ tablespoon light brown sugar, or to taste
$\frac{1}{4}$ cup *each* chopped dates and chopped nuts

In a medium-size bowl, whisk yogurt cheese, orange peel and sugar until well blended. Stir in the dates and nuts. Cover and chill until serving time. Makes about 1$\frac{1}{4}$ cups.

Per 1/4 cup: Calories 100; protein 5 gm; carbohydrates 12 gm; fat 4 gm; cholesterol 0 mg; calcium 211 mg; sodium 33 mg. Exchanges: 1/2 skim milk and 1 fat.

Honey-Date Spread

1 cup non-fat yogurt cheese
2 tablespoons honey
1 teaspoon lemon juice
  Dash cinnamon
$\frac{1}{4}$ cup chopped dates

In a medium-size bowl, combine yogurt cheese, honey, lemon juice and cinnamon; whisk until smooth and well blended. Stir in the dates. Cover and chill until serving time. Makes about 1 cup.

Per 1/4 cup: Calories 103; protein 5 gm; carbohydrates 21 gm; fat <1 gm; cholesterol 0 mg; calcium 145 mg; sodium 41 mg. Exchanges: 1 fruit and 1/2 skim milk.

7 • FROM THE BAKERY

If you know you shouldn't be snacking on baked goods, these recipes will be a real treat.

Most of them are low in fat and cholesterol. And though they're not strictly low-calorie, they're a lot lower than traditional versions. The recipes are arranged by calorie count from lowest to highest; only you know how far you can go . . . .

And if you yearn for frosting, top your slice of cake with plain vanilla yogurt cheese or frost with one of the toppings in Chapter Six.

Baked Corn Chips

5-inch corn tortillas, as thin as you can find

Preheat oven to 350°.

Using a knife or kitchen scissors, cut each tortilla into 8 wedges. Place in a single layer on an ungreased baking sheet.

Bake about 15 to 20 minutes until crisp. Cool. Store in a closed container.

Variation. Use 6-inch flour tortillas, and cut each wedge into small pieces.

Per corn tortilla (8 pieces): Calories 45; protein 1 gm; carbohydrates 8 gm; fat 1 gm; cholesterol 0 mg; calcium 40 mg; sodium 25 mg. Exchanges: 1/2 starch/bread.

Per flour tortilla: Calories 75; protein 2 gm; carbohydrates 13 gm; fat 2 gm; cholesterol 0 mg; calcium 56 mg; sodium 131 mg. Exchanges: 1 starch/bread.

Baked Pita Chips

1 5-inch round pita bread (pocket bread)

Preheat oven to 350°.

Split pita into 2 rounds. Cut each round into 8 wedges. Place in a single layer on a cookie sheet. Bake about 8 to 10 minutes, until crisp. Cool.

Store in a closed container.

4 wedges: Calories 35; protein 3 gm; carbohydrates 8 gm; fat 0; cholesterol 0 mg; calcium not available; sodium 80 mg. Exchanges: 1/2 starch/bread.

• **Variation.** Brush lightly with oil and sprinkle with your choice of seasoning, such as garlic powder or blended herb mix.

Basic Dough

Look, no yeast! Makes great pizza crust,
breadsticks, twists, rolls, Danish and sticky buns.

2¹/₂ cups all-purpose flour*
  2 teaspoons baking powder
¹/₄ teaspoon salt, optional
¹/₂ teaspoon baking soda
  2 large egg whites
  1 cup non-fat yogurt cheese
  6 tablespoons light margarine, melted and cooled

Sift flour, baking powder, salt and baking soda together.

In another bowl, combine egg whites, yogurt cheese and margarine, and whisk until well blended. Add dry ingredients and stir to form a smooth dough.

Turn the dough out onto a floured surface and knead for 30 seconds.

*¹/₂ cup whole wheat flour may be substituted for ¹/₂ cup of the all-purpose flour.

Diet note: To lower sodium, use low-sodium baking powder.

Mini Hors d'Oeuvres Buns

1 recipe Basic Dough *(recipe, page 140)*
½ egg white, lightly beaten

Preheat oven to 450°.

Roll dough into a rope about 2 inches thick and cut cross-wise into 32 pieces.

Roll each piece into a small ball. Flatten slightly. Place on an ungreased baking sheet and brush with beaten egg white. Bake in upper third of oven for about 15 minutes or until golden (check after 12 minutes to see that they are not browning too much).

Makes 32.

1 bun (all-purpose flour). Calories 49; protein 2 gm; carbohydrates 8 gm; fat 1 gm; cholesterol 0 mg; calcium 35 mg; sodium 67 mg. Exchanges: 1/2 starch/bread.

1 bun (flour combination): Calories 48; protein 2 gm; carbohydrates 7 gm; fat 1 gm; cholesterol 0 mg; calcium 35 mg; sodium 67 mg. Exchanges: 1/2 starch/bread.

Oatmeal Kisses

3 cups rolled oats (old fashioned or quick)
1 cup unsifted all-purpose flour
1 teaspoon ground cinnamon
$^1/_4$ teaspoon baking soda
$^1/_8$ teaspoon ground nutmeg
$^3/_4$ cup chopped nuts or raisins, optional
1 cup firmly packed light brown sugar
$^3/_4$ cup non-fat yogurt cheese
2 egg whites
2 teaspoons vanilla extract

Preheat the oven to 350°. Spray cookie sheets with non-stick cooking spray.

In a large bowl, stir together oats, flour, cinnamon, baking soda, nutmeg and nuts.

In a medium-size bowl, combine the brown sugar, yogurt cheese, egg whites and vanilla and whisk until smooth. Stir into the dry ingredients and mix well.

Drop by level tablespoonfuls onto prepared cookie sheets, flattening dough slightly with back of spoon. Bake 10 to 12 minutes or until lightly browned. Remove immediately from cookie sheets and cool on racks.

Makes about 4 dozen.

2 cookies: Calories 99; protein 3 gm; carbohydrates 20 gm; fat 1 gm; cholesterol 0 mg; calcium 33 mg; sodium 21 mg. Exchanges: 1 fruit and 1/2 skim milk.

Whole Wheat Muffins

$1/2$ cup whole wheat flour
$1/3$ cup all-purpose flour
  1 teaspoon baking powder
$1/4$ teaspoon baking soda
$1/4$ teaspoon caraway seeds
$1/2$ teaspoon poppy seeds
$1/4$ teaspoon salt
  3 tablespoons chopped walnuts, optional
$1/2$ cup non-fat yogurt cheese
  2 tablespoons water
  2 egg whites
  1 tablespoon vegetable oil
  1 tablespoon honey

Preheat oven to 400°. Spray 12 miniature muffin cups with non-stick cooking spray.

In a medium-size bowl, combine flours, baking powder, baking soda, caraway seeds, poppy seeds, salt and walnuts.

In a small bowl, combine the yogurt cheese, water, egg whites, oil and honey, and whisk until well blended. Add to the dry ingredients and stir until just moistened.

Spoon into muffin cups and bake for 15 minutes.

Makes 12.

Per muffin: Calories 54; protein 2 gm; carbohydrates 8 gm; fat 1 gm; cholesterol 0 mg; calcium 49 mg; sodium 104 mg. Exchanges: 1/2 starch/bread.

Diet note: To lower sodium, eliminate salt and use low-sodium baking powder.

Carrot Cake

$3/4$ cup non-fat yogurt cheese
4 egg whites
1 teaspoon vanilla extract
$1/2$ cup *each* whole wheat flour and all-purpose flour
$1/2$ cup light brown sugar
1 teaspoon baking powder
1 teaspoon baking soda
1 teaspoon cinnamon
$1/4$ teaspoon salt, or to taste
$1^1/2$ cups (about 7 oz.) finely shredded carrots
$1/2$ cup chopped nuts, optional

Preheat oven to 350°. Spray an 8 x 8-inch square baking pan with non-stick cooking spray.

In a large bowl, whisk the yogurt cheese, egg whites and vanilla until smooth.

In another bowl combine the flours, sugar, baking powder, baking soda, cinnamon and salt. Add yogurt mixture, carrots and nuts, and blend well.

Spread evenly in pan and bake for about 30 minutes or until the cake tests done. Cool on a rack before cutting into 2-inch squares.

Makes 16 squares.

Per square: Calories 70; protein 3 gm; carbohydrates 15 gm; fat <1 gm; cholesterol 0 mg; calcium 55 mg; sodium 132 mg. Exchanges: 1 starch/bread.

Whole Wheat Pancakes

1 cup non-fat yogurt cheese
4 egg whites
2 tablespoons melted margarine, cooled
1½ tablespoons honey
⅔ cup all-purpose flour
⅓ cup whole wheat flour
1½ teaspoons baking soda
½ teaspoon baking powder

In a medium-size bowl, whisk yogurt cheese, egg whites, margarine and honey until smooth.

In another bowl, sift flours, baking soda and baking powder. Add to the yogurt cheese mixture and whisk until smooth.

Preheat griddle and spray with non-stick cooking spray. Using a 1/4 cup measuring cup, pour batter onto the griddle and spread with a spatula into a 4-inch round (mixture will be very thick). Cook until bubbles form and the pancake is brown. Turn and brown other side.

Makes about 12 four-inch pancakes.

Per pancake: Calories 78; protein 4 gm; carbohydrates 11 gm; fat 2 gm; cholesterol 0 mg; calcium 61 mg; sodium 171 mg. Exchanges: 1 starch/bread.

Diet note: To reduce sodium, use low-sodium baking powder.

Pumpkin Bread

This is not sweet. You may wish to double the honey.

    1 cup non-fat yogurt cheese
    1 stick (4 oz.) light margarine, softened
  1/2 cup honey
    2 eggs + 4 egg whites
    1 can (16 oz.) pumpkin
    2 cups all-purpose flour
1 1/2 cups whole wheat flour
    2 teaspoons baking soda
    1 teaspoon cinnamon
  1/2 teaspoon *each* baking powder and salt
  1/4 teaspoon ground cloves
    1 cup chopped nuts, optional

Preheat the oven to 350°. Spray two 9 x 5-inch loaf pans with non-stick cooking spray.

In a large bowl, beat yogurt cheese, margarine and honey until fluffy. Add the eggs, egg whites and pumpkin; beat well. Mixture may look curdled.

In a medium-size bowl, combine dry ingredients and stir well. Add to the pumpkin mixture and stir until just moistened. Fold in nuts. Divide between the 2 pans and bake for about 70 minutes or until bread tests done.

Cool 15 minutes on a rack, then remove from pans.

Makes 32 slices, 16 per loaf.

Per slice: Calories 90; protein 3 gm; carbohydrates 16 gm; fat 2 gm; cholesterol 17 mg; calcium 33 mg; sodium 141 mg. Exchanges: 1 starch/bread.

Diet note: To reduce sodium, eliminate salt and use low-sodium baking powder. To reduce cholesterol, use 2 egg whites for each whole egg.

Pizza Crust

1 recipe Basic Dough *(recipe, page 140)*

Preheat the oven to 450°.
Divide dough into 2 equal parts. Roll out each piece on a lightly floured surface with a rolling pin, patting into a 10-inch round. Place on ungreased pizza pans or baking sheets and push edges up a bit to form a base.
Top with your favorite pizza topping and bake for about 15 to 20 minutes or until browned.
Cut each pizza into 8 wedges.
Makes 16 pieces, 8 per pizza.

1 wedge without topping (all-purpose flour): Calories 97: protein 3 gm; carbohydrates 15 gm; fat 2 gm; cholesterol 0 mg; calcium 69 mg; sodium 133 mg. Exchanges: 1 starch/bread.

1 wedge without topping (flour combination): Calories 96; protein 4 gm; carbohydrates 15 gm; fat 2 gm; cholesterol 0 mg; calcium 70 mg; sodium 133 mg. Exchanges: 1 starch/bread.

Twists

1 recipe Basic Dough *(recipe, page 140)*
½ egg white, lightly beaten
   Seeds (sesame, poppy, caraway or dill), optional

Preheat oven to 450°.

On a lightly floured surface, roll dough into a rope about 2 inches thick and cut crosswise into 16 pieces.

Roll each piece into a rope about 8 inches long, tapering the ends slightly.

Fold each rope loosely in half and twist it twice, pinching the ends together. Place on an ungreased baking sheet, brush with beaten egg white and sprinkle with seeds. Bake in upper third of oven for about 15 minutes or until golden.

Makes 16.

1 twist (all-purpose flour): Calories 97; protein 4 gm; carbohydrates 15 gm; fat 2 gm; cholesterol 0 mg; calcium 69 mg; sodium 134 mg. Exchanges: 1 starch/bread.

1 twist (flour combination): Calories 97; protein 4 gm; carbohydrates 15 gm; fat 2 gm; cholesterol 0 mg; calcium 70 mg; sodium 135 mg. Exchanges: 1 starch/bread.

Breadsticks

1 recipe Basic Dough *(recipe, page 140)*
$1/2$ egg white, lightly beaten
    Seeds (sesame, poppy, caraway or dill), optional

Preheat oven to 450°.

On a lightly floured surface, roll dough into a rope about 2 inches thick and cut crosswise into 16 pieces.

Roll each piece into a breadstick about 8 inches long, tapering the ends slightly.

Place on an ungreased baking sheet, brush with the beaten egg white and sprinkle with seeds. Bake in upper third of oven for about 15 minutes or until golden.

Makes 16.

1 breadstick (all-purpose flour): Calories 97; protein 4 gm; carbohydrates 15 gm; fat 2 gm; cholesterol 0 mg; calcium 69 mg; sodium 134 mg. Exchanges: 1 starch/bread.

1 breadstick (flour combination): Calories 97; protein 4 gm; carbohydrates 15 gm; fat 2 gm; cholesterol 0 mg; calcium 70 mg; sodium 135 mg. Exchanges: 1 starch/bread.

Bagels

"Egg" bagels without the cholesterol.

1 recipe Basic Dough *(recipe, page 140)*
$^1/_2$ egg white, lightly beaten
    Seeds (sesame, poppy, caraway or dill), optional

Preheat oven to 450°.

On a lightly floured surface, roll dough into a rope about 2 inches thick and cut crosswise into 16 pieces.

Roll each piece into a rope about 8 inches long, tapering the ends slightly.

Form each rope into a ring, pinching the ends together.

Place on an ungreased baking sheet, brush with beaten egg white and sprinkle with seeds. Bake in upper third of oven for about 15 minutes or until golden.

Makes 16.

• **Suggestion.** Spread bagels with yogurt cheese instead of cream cheese. (Check nutritional table *(page 177);* you'll be amazed at the difference in fat and calories!)

---

1 bagel (all-purpose flour). Calories 97; protein 4 gm; carbohydrates 15 gm; fat 2 gm; cholesterol 0 mg; calcium 69 mg; sodium 134 mg. Exchanges: 1 starch/bread.

1 bagel (flour combination): Calories 97; protein 4 gm; carbohydrates 15 gm; fat 2 gm; cholesterol 0 mg; calcium 70 mg; sodium 135 mg. Exchanges: 1 starch/bread.

Soft Pretzels

1 recipe Basic Dough *(recipe, page 140)*
$^1/_2$ egg white, lightly beaten
  Coarse salt, optional

Preheat oven to 450°.

On a lightly floured surface, roll dough into a rope about 2 inches thick and cut crosswise into 16 pieces.

Roll each piece into a rope about 8 inches long, tapering the ends slightly.

Form into a knot, brush with beaten egg white and sprinkle with salt. Place on an ungreased baking sheet. Bake in upper third of oven for about 15 minutes or until golden.

Makes 16.

1 pretzel (all-purpose flour). Calories 97; protein 4 gm; carbohydrates 15 gm; fat 2 gm; cholesterol 0 mg; calcium 69 mg; sodium 134 mg. Exchanges: 1 starch/bread.

1 pretzel (flour combination): Calories 97; protein 4 gm; carbohydrates 15 gm; fat 2 gm; cholesterol 0 mg; calcium 70 mg; sodium 135 mg. Exchanges: 1 starch/bread.

Lemon Cheesecake

2 cups non-fat yogurt cheese
$1/4$ cup + 3 tablespoons sugar, or to taste
1 tablespoon cornstarch
4 egg whites
   Juice of 1 lemon
1 teaspoon vanilla
$1/2$ teaspoon grated lemon peel, or $1/4$ teaspoon lemon extract

Preheat oven to 325°. Spray an 8-inch pie pan or 7-inch springform pan with non-stick cooking spray.

In a large bowl, whisk together yogurt cheese, sugar and cornstarch. Lightly beat egg whites, and add to yogurt cheese mixture with lemon juice, vanilla and lemon peel. Whisk until well blended.

Pour into prepared pan and smooth the top with a spatula. Bake until center is set: 20 to 25 minutes for a pie pan, or 45 to 55 minutes for a springform.

Cool slightly on a wire rack. Refrigerate until chilled.

Serves 8.

Per slice: Calories 100; protein 6 gm; carbohydrates 18 gm; fat <1 gm; cholesterol 0 mg; calcium 143 mg; sodium 65 mg. Exchanges: 1 fruit and 1/2 skim milk.

• **Variation.** For a quick lemon cheesecake, make the yogurt cheese from lemon yogurt. Follow the recipe, omitting sugar, lemon juice and vanilla.

Crescents

Use any type of filling: sweet, savory,
spinach, cheese, etc.

1 recipe Basic Dough *(recipe, page 140)*
5 tablespoons preserves (made without sugar)
½ egg white, lightly beaten

Preheat oven to 450°.

On a lightly floured surface, roll out dough 1/8 inch thick and cut into 3-inch rounds.

Place about 1 teaspoon filling in each center, moisten the edge with water and fold over and pinch to seal.

Place on ungreased baking sheet. Chill 20 minutes, then brush with the beaten egg white. Bake in upper third of oven for about 15 minutes or until golden.

Makes 16.

1 crescent (all-purpose flour). Calories 103; protein 4 gm; carbohydrates 17 gm; fat 2 gm; cholesterol 0 mg; calcium 70 mg; sodium 141 mg. Exchanges: 1 starch/bread and 1/2 fruit.

1 crescent (flour combination): Calories 102; protein 4 gm; carbohydrates 16 gm; fat 2 gm; cholesterol 0 mg; calcium 71 mg; sodium 141 mg. Exchanges: 1 starch/bread and 1/2 fruit.

Danish Pastry

1 recipe Basic Dough *(recipe, page 140)*
6 tablespoons preserves (made without sugar)

Preheat oven to 450°.

On a lightly floured surface, roll dough into a rope about 2 inches thick and cut crosswise into 16 pieces.

Roll each piece into a rope about 8 inches long, tapering the ends slightly.

Form each rope into a coil, flattening the center into a little hollow. Fill hollow with about 1 heaping teaspoon of preserves.

Place on an ungreased baking sheet. Bake in upper third of oven for about 15 minutes or until golden.

Makes 16.

1 pastry (all-purpose flour). Calories 104; protein 3 gm; carbohydrates 17 gm; fat 2 gm; cholesterol 0 mg; calcium 70 mg; sodium 141 mg. Exchanges: 1 starch/bread and 1/2 fruit.

1 pastry (flour combination): Calories 103; protein 4 gm; carbohydrates 17 gm; fat 2 gm; cholesterol 0 mg; calcium 71 mg; sodium 141 mg. Exchanges: 1 starch/bread and 1/2 fruit.

> • *Easy Danish #1.* Spread non-fat yogurt cheese on a toasted English muffin half. Sprinkle with cinnamon sugar, and toast under the broiler.
>
> • *Easy Danish #2.* Spread a toasted muffin half with yogurt cheese made from vanilla or lemon yogurt. Place a spoonful of preserves in the center. Toast under the broiler.

Gingerbread

Rich-tasting!

$^3/_4$ cup whole wheat flour

$^1/_2$ teaspoon *each* ground ginger and ground cinnamon

$^1/_2$ teaspoon baking soda

$^1/_8$ teaspoon ground cloves

2 tablespoons + 2 teaspoons light margarine, melted

$^1/_2$ cup non-fat yogurt cheese

$^1/_4$ cup light brown sugar

2 egg whites

2 tablespoons molasses

Preheat the oven to 350°. Spray an 8 x 4-inch loaf pan with non-stick cooking spray.

In a large bowl combine the flour, ginger, cinnamon, baking soda and cloves.

In a small bowl, whisk remaining ingredients until smooth and well blended. Add to dry ingredients and whisk until smooth.

Transfer to the pan and bake 25 to 30 minutes or until cake tests done. Cool on a rack before cutting into 2-inch squares.

Makes 8 squares.

Per square: Calories 107; protein 4 gm; carbohydrates 19 gm; fat 2 gm; cholesterol 0 mg; calcium 64 mg; sodium 124 mg. Exchanges: 1 starch/bread and 1/2 skim milk.

Peanut Butter Bran Muffins

  1 cup bran
$^1/_2$ cup golden raisins
$^1/_4$ cup rolled oats (quick or old-fashioned)
$^1/_4$ cup wheat germ
$^1/_2$ cup boiling water
$^3/_4$ cup all-purpose flour
$^1/_2$ cup whole wheat flour
1$^1/_4$ teaspoons baking soda
$^1/_4$ teaspoon salt
  1 cup non-fat yogurt cheese
$^1/_3$ cup honey
  2 egg whites
  3 tablespoons *each* molasses and chunky peanut butter
  1 tablespoon safflower oil

Preheat oven to 375°. Prepare 20 muffin cups with paper liners or spray with non-stick cooking spray.

Combine bran, raisins, oats and wheat germ in a medium-size bowl. Add boiling water and allow to soften for 5 minutes.

Sift all-purpose flour, whole wheat flour, baking soda and salt into a large bowl.

In a medium-size bowl, whisk yogurt cheese, honey, egg whites, molasses, peanut butter and oil until well blended. Stir in bran mixture. Add to dry ingredients and stir until just moistened.

Fill each muffin cup about three-fourths full. Bake for about 25 minutes.

Makes 20.

Per muffin: Calories 110; protein 4 gm; carbohydrates 21 gm; fat 2 gm; cholesterol 0; calcium 46 mg; sodium 128 mg. Exchanges: 1 starch/bread and 1/2 skim milk.

Diet note: To lower sodium, eliminate salt and use no-salt added peanut butter.

Chili Cornbread

1 cup (4 oz.) grated sharp Cheddar cheese
1 tablespoon chili powder
1 cup yellow cornmeal
2 teaspoons baking powder
1/4 teaspoon salt
3 large egg whites
1/2 cup non-fat yogurt cheese
1/4 cup water
1/3 cup vegetable oil
1 can (8 3/4 oz.) cream-style corn (low-sodium)

Preheat oven to 300°. Spray an 8 x 8-inch baking pan with non-stick cooking spray.

In a small bowl, stir together the Cheddar cheese and chili powder. Set aside.

Combine cornmeal, baking powder and salt in a large bowl.

In a medium-size bowl, combine the egg whites, yogurt cheese, water and oil, and whisk until blended. Stir in the corn. Add to the cornmeal mixture and and stir until just moistened.

Pour half the batter into baking pan. Sprinkle with half the Cheddar cheese mixture. Repeat layers.

Bake for about 40 minutes or until bread tests done. Let stand for 10 minutes before cutting into two-inch squares.

Makes 16 squares.

Per square: Calories 121; protein 4 gm; carbohydrates 11 gm; fat 7 gm; cholesterol 8 mg; calcium 102 mg; sodium 137 mg. Exchanges: 1 starch/bread and 1 fat.

Diet note: Low-fat and/or low-sodium Cheddar cheese may be substituted, although the flavor will be milder. To lower sodium, eliminate salt and use low-sodium baking powder.

Mixed Grain Cornbread

Goes well with the fruit spreads in Chapter 6.

$1/3$ cup yellow cornmeal
$1/3$ cup whole wheat flour
$1/3$ cup wheat germ
  1 tablespoon baking powder
  4 egg whites
$1/4$ cup safflower oil
$1/4$ cup honey
  1 cup non-fat yogurt cheese

Preheat oven to 350°. Spray a 9-inch round pan with non-stick cooking spray.

In a large bowl, combine the cornmeal, whole wheat flour, wheat germ and baking powder.

In a small bowl, combine egg whites, oil, honey and yogurt cheese, and whisk until smooth. Add to the dry ingredients and stir until just moistened.

Pour into the pan and bake for 35 minutes. Serve warm, cut into wedges.

Makes 12 wedges.

1 wedge: Calories 122; protein 4 gm; carbohydrates 15 gm; fat 5 gm; cholesterol 0 mg; calcium 113 mg; sodium 106 mg. Exchanges: 1 starch/bread and 1 fat.

Diet note: To reduce sodium, low-sodium baking powder may be used.

Corn Muffins

1 cup yellow cornmeal

1 cup all-purpose flour

3 tablespoons light brown sugar

1 tablespoon baking powder

$1/4$ teaspoon salt

$3/4$ cup non-fat yogurt cheese

2 egg whites

$1/4$ cup corn oil

$1/4$ cup water

Preheat oven to 425°. Prepare 12 muffin cups with paper liners or spray with non-stick cooking spray.

Combine cornmeal, flour, sugar, baking powder and salt in a large bowl.

In a medium-size bowl, combine the yogurt cheese, egg whites, oil and water, and whisk until well blended. Add to the dry ingredients and stir until just moistened.

Fill muffin cups about three-fourths full. Bake 15 to 18 minutes, or until golden brown.

Makes 12.

Per muffin: Calories 131; protein 4 gm; carbohydrates 18 gm; fat 5 gm; cholesterol 0 mg; calcium 98 mg; sodium 143 mg. Exchanges: 1 starch/bread and 1 fat.

Diet note: To reduce sodium, eliminate salt and use low-sodium baking powder.

Blueberry Oat Muffins

2½ cups rolled oats (quick or old-fashioned)
½ cup firmly packed dark brown sugar
2 teaspoons baking powder
½ teaspoon cinnamon
½ teaspoon grated lemon peel
¼ teaspoon salt, or to taste
1 cup fresh blueberries
2 egg whites
⅔ cup non-fat yogurt cheese
2 tablespoons vegetable oil
3 tablespoons water

Preheat oven to 400°. Prepare 12 muffin cups with paper liners or spray with non-stick cooking spray.

In a food processor (metal blade) or blender, process oats about 1 minute. Transfer to a large bowl and add brown sugar, baking powder, cinnamon, lemon peel and salt. Stir in the blueberries.

Whisk the egg whites in a small bowl until foamy. Add the yogurt cheese, oil and water, and whisk until well blended. Add to the dry ingredients and stir until just moistened.

Fill muffin cups almost full. Bake 20 to 22 minutes, or until golden brown.

Makes 12.

Per muffin: Calories 139; protein 4 gm; carbohydrates 23 gm; fat 3 gm; cholesterol 0 mg; calcium 90 mg; sodium 119 mg. Exchanges: 1 starch/bread and 1 fruit.

Diet note: To lower sodium, eliminate salt and use low-sodium baking powder.

Banana Bread

1 cup non-fat yogurt cheese
$\frac{1}{2}$ cup light brown sugar, firmly packed
$\frac{1}{2}$ stick (4 Tbsp.) light margarine, melted
2 medium-size ripe bananas, mashed
4 egg whites
1 cup all-purpose flour
$\frac{3}{4}$ cup oat bran
$\frac{1}{2}$ cup whole wheat flour
2 teaspoons baking powder
$\frac{1}{2}$ teaspoon baking soda
$\frac{1}{2}$ cup raisins or chopped dates

Preheat the oven to 350°. Spray a 9 x 5-inch loaf pan with non-stick cooking spray.

In large bowl (or food processor), combine yogurt cheese, sugar and margarine; whisk (or process) until smooth. Beat in bananas and egg whites.

Combine dry ingredients and raisins in a large bowl. Add the yogurt cheese mixture and blend until just moistened.

Transfer to pan and bake 60 to 70 minutes, or until bread tests done. Cool 10 minutes on rack before removing from pan or cutting. Makes 16 slices.

- **Banana Muffins.** Spoon batter into 16 paper-lined muffin cups, two-thirds full. Bake at 350° for 20 to 25 minutes.

Per slice/muffin: Calories 141; protein 4 gm; carbohydrates 27 gm; fat 2 gm; cholesterol 0 mg; calcium 82 mg; sodium 125 mg. Exchanges: 1 starch/bread and 1 fruit.

Sticky Buns

1 recipe Basic Dough *(recipe, page 140)*
16 teaspoons melted light margarine
8 tablespoons dark brown sugar
Chopped nuts, optional
$^1/_3$ cup raisins
$^1/_2$ teaspoon cinnamon

Preheat oven to 450°.

Spray 16 muffin cups with non-stick cooking spray. Place 1 teaspoon melted margarine in each cup, then sprinkle with 1/2 tablespoon sugar. Add a few nuts if desired.

Knead raisins and cinnamon into Basic Dough on a lightly floured surface. Roll into a rope about 2 inches thick and cut crosswise into 16 pieces.

Roll each piece into a rope about 8 inches long, tapering the ends slightly.

Form each rope into a coil and place in muffin cups. Bake in upper third of oven for about 15 minutes or until golden.

Makes 16.

1 bun (all-purpose flour). Calories 150; protein 4 gm; carbohydrates 24 gm; fat 4 gm; cholesterol 0 mg; calcium 78 mg; sodium 181 mg. Exchanges: 1 starch/bread, 1/2 fruit and 1 fat.

1 bun (flour combination): Calories 149; protein 4 gm; carbohydrates 24 gm; fat 4 gm; cholesterol 0 mg; calcium 79 mg; sodium 182 mg. Exchanges: 1 starch/bread, 1/2 fruit and 1 fat.

Applesauce Spice Cake

1 cup non-fat yogurt cheese

1¼ cups unsweetened applesauce

3 egg whites (just under ½ cup)

1 teaspoon vanilla

1½ cups *each* all-purpose flour and whole wheat flour

¾ cup light brown sugar

½ cup raisins

2 tablespoons oat bran

2 teaspoons *each* baking powder and baking soda

2 teaspoons ground cinnamon

½ teaspoon salt, optional

½ teaspoon ground nutmeg

¼ teaspoon allspice

Preheat oven to 350°. Spray a 9 x 13-inch baking pan with non-stick cooking spray.

In a large bowl, whisk the yogurt cheese, applesauce, egg whites and vanilla until well blended.

In another large bowl, combine the dry ingredients. Add to the applesauce mixture and beat well. Pour into pan and bake 35 to 45 minutes or until the cake tests done.

Cool slightly on a rack before cutting.

Makes 15 squares.

Per slice: Calories 168 protein 5 gm; carbohydrates 37 gm; fat 1 gm; cholesterol 0 mg; calcium 90 mg; sodium 177 mg. Exchanges: 2 starch/bread.

Great Granola Bars

An after-school or lunchbox treat.

2 cups old-fashioned rolled oats
1 cup light brown sugar, firmly packed
1 cup dry roasted unsalted peanuts, coarsely chopped
$^1/_2$ cup raisins
$^1/_2$ cup non-fat yogurt cheese
$^1/_2$ cup egg whites (3 or 4)
1 teaspoon vanilla extract

Preheat oven to 350°. Spray a 9 x 9-inch baking pan with non-stick cooking spray.

Combine rolled oats, brown sugar, peanuts and raisins in a large bowl.

In another bowl, whisk the yogurt cheese, egg whites and vanilla until well blended. Stir into the dry ingredients.

Press mixture firmly into the baking pan and bake about 30 minutes or until lightly browned. Cool on rack for 10 minutes before cutting into bars.

Makes 16 bars.

Per bar: Calories 168; protein 5 gm; carbohydrates 28 gm; fat 5 gm; cholesterol 0 mg; calcium 46 mg; sodium 21 mg. Exchanges: 1 starch/bread, 1/2 skim milk and 1 fat.

Diet note: To lower calories and fat, reduce or eliminate the nuts.

Sandwich Buns

1 recipe Basic Dough *(recipe, page 140)*

$1/2$ egg white, lightly beaten

Preheat oven to 450°.

On a lightly floured surface, roll dough into a rope about 2 inches thick and cut crosswise into 8 pieces.

Roll each piece in a ball. Flatten slightly. Place on an ungreased baking sheet and brush with beaten egg white. Bake in upper third of oven for about 25 minutes or until golden.

Makes 8.

1 bun (all-purpose flour). Calories 195; protein 7 gm; carbohydrates 30 gm; fat 5 gm; cholesterol 0 mg; calcium 139 mg; sodium 269 mg. Exchanges: 2 starch/breads and 1 fat.

1 bun (flour combination): Calories 193; protein 7 gm; carbohydrates 30 gm; fat 5 gm; cholesterol 0 mg; calcium 140 mg; sodium 269 mg. Exchanges: 2 starch/breads and 1 fat.

Waffles

1 cup all-purpose flour
1 cup old-fashioned rolled oats
$^1/_2$ cup yellow cornmeal
5 teaspoons baking powder
2 cups non-fat yogurt cheese
$^3/_4$ cup water
6 tablespoons light margarine, melted, or oil
3 large egg whites

In a large bowl, combine the flour, oats, cornmeal and baking powder.

In another large bowl, whisk the yogurt cheese, water, margarine and egg whites until well combined. Stir into dry ingredients and allow to stand for 15 minutes.

Preheat a waffle iron on medium setting and pour batter to cover about two-thirds of grid. Bake until steam stops escaping and waffles are golden, 3 to 4 minutes.

Makes six 7-inch waffles.

Per waffle: Calories 279; protein 13 gm; carbohydrates 39 gm; fat 7 gm; cholesterol 0 mg; calcium 401 mg; sodium 477 mg. Exchanges: 2 starch/bread, 1/2 lowfat milk and 1 fat.

Diet note: To lower sodium, use low-sodium baking powder.

8 • ICE CREAM TREATS

Ice cream is always a popular snack, but the rich creamy sort is "out" for most people.

When you're watching fat and calories there's not much left but grainier ice milks. Sorbets are good, but sometimes you wish for something richer.

With the discovery of yogurt cheese, you can now have thick creamy "yogurt" ice cream that has almost no fat! The choice of sweetener will be up to you, based on your individual dietary needs.

In addition to the recipes in this chapter, think of all the other possibilities: fresh raspberry, fresh peach, chocolate mint, mocha . . . .

Vanilla Ice Cream

1 cup nonfat yogurt cheese
2 tablespoons sugar or other sweetener
$1/2$ teaspoon vanilla extract

Combine ingredients. Place in an ice cream maker and follow manufacturer's directions.
Makes 2 servings.

Per serving: Calories 132; protein 9 gm; carbohydrates 21 gm; fat <1 gm; cholesterol 0 mg; calcium 280 mg; sodium 80 mg. Exchanges: 1/2 fruit and 1 skim milk.

• *Variation.* Use vanilla yogurt; omit sugar and vanilla.

Lemon Ice Cream

1 cup nonfat yogurt cheese
2 tablespoons sugar or other sweetener
Juice of ¹/₂ lemon

Combine ingredients. Place in an ice cream maker and follow manufacturer's directions.
Makes 2 servings.

Per serving: Calories 134; protein 10 gm; carbohydrates 23 gm; fat <1 gm; cholesterol 0 mg; calcium 282 mg; sodium 80 mg. Exchanges: 1/2 fruit and 1 skim milk.

• *Variation.* Use lemon yogurt; omit sugar and lemon juice.

Fruit Ice Cream Softies

You can have a lot of fun with these, mixing and matching fruits and extracts. Any kind of sweetener can be used. Berries and other fresh fruit can be bought when seasonal and kept in premeasured portions in the freezer.

BASIC RECIPE

2 cups fresh or canned fruit, in chunks
    Lemon juice or ascorbic acid power (to prevent fruits such as bananas, apples, peaches or pears from turning brown)
$1/4$ teaspoon flavoring extract, optional
$1/4$ cup sweetener, or to taste (depends on sweetness of fruit)
1 cup non-fat yogurt cheese

Arrange fruit on a baking sheet lined with waxed paper. Place in the freezer for about 4 hours.

In a food processor (metal blade), process frozen fruit until powdery. Add remaining ingredients and process until thick and smooth. Do not overprocess.

Spoon into 4 small bowls and serve immediately. To hold, place in freezer and remove 30 minutes before serving.

• **Frozen Yogurt Bars.** Spoon any Ice Cream Softie mixture into paper cups, insert sticks, and place in freezer.

Pineapple Ice Cream Softie

2 cups fresh pineapple chunks (or canned, drained)
1/4 cup confectioners' sugar, optional
1/4 teaspoon vanilla or coconut extract
1 cup non-fat yogurt cheese

Arrange fruit on a baking sheet lined with waxed paper. Place in the freezer for about 4 hours.

In food processor, process frozen pineapple until powdery. Add remaining ingredients and process until thick and smooth. Do not overprocess.

Spoon into 4 dessert bowls and serve immediately.*

Serves 4.

*To hold, place in freezer; remove 30 minutes before serving.

Per serving: Calories 79; protein 5 gm; carbohydrates 14 gm; fat <1 gm; cholesterol 0 mg; calcium 146 mg; sodium 41 mg. Exchanges: 1/2 fruit and 1/2 skim milk.

Strawberry Ice Cream Softie

2 cups small strawberries
$1/4$ teaspoon vanilla extract
$1/8$ cup honey
1 cup non-fat yogurt cheese

Arrange strawberries on a baking sheet lined with waxed paper. Place in the freezer for about 4 hours.

In a food processor, process frozen strawberries until powdery. Add remaining ingredients and process until thick and smooth. Do not overprocess.

Spoon into 4 dessert bowls and serve immediately.*
Serves 4.

*To hold, place in freezer; remove 30 minutes before serving.

Per serving: Calories 95; protein 5 gm; carbohydrates 18 gm; fat <1 gm; cholesterol 0 mg; calcium 151 mg; sodium 42 mg. Exchanges: 1 fruit and 1/2 skim milk.

Blackberry Ice Cream Softie

12 ounces blackberries
1 cup non-fat yogurt cheese
1/8 cup honey

    Arrange berries on a baking sheet lined with waxed paper. Place in the freezer for about 4 hours.

    In a food processor, process frozen blackberries until powdery. Add remaining ingredients and process until thick and smooth. Do not overprocess.

    Spoon into 4 dessert bowls and serve immediately.*

    Serves 4.

*To hold, place in freezer; remove 30 minutes before serving.

Per serving: Calories 115; protein 5 gm; carbohydrates 24 gm; fat <1 gm; cholesterol 0 mg; calcium 167 mg; sodium 41 mg. Exchanges: 1 fruit and 1/2 skim milk.

Cranberry Ice Cream Softie

2 cups fresh cranberries
1 cup non-fat yogurt cheese
$1/4$ cup maple syrup
$1/4$ teaspoon orange extract

Arrange cranberries on a baking sheet lined with waxed paper. Place in the freezer for about 4 hours.

In a food processor, process frozen cranberries until powdery. Add remaining ingredients and process until thick and smooth. Do not overprocess.

Spoon into 4 dessert bowls and serve immediately.*
Serves 4.

*To hold, place in freezer; remove 30 minutes before serving.

Per serving: Calories 115; protein 5 gm; carbohydrates 23 gm; fat <1 gm; cholesterol 0 mg; calcium 164 mg; sodium 43 mg. Exchanges: 1 fruit and 1/2 skim milk.

Pear Ice Cream Softie

2 cups fresh pear chunks, peeled
1 tablespoon lemon juice
$1/4$ teaspoon vanilla or coconut extract
$1/8$ cup honey
1 cup non-fat yogurt cheese

Arrange pears on a baking sheet lined with waxed paper. Sprinkle with lemon juice to keep from discoloring. Place in the freezer for about 4 hours.

In a food processor (metal blade), process frozen pears until powdery. Add the remaining ingredients and process until thick and smooth. Do not overprocess.

Spoon into 4 dessert bowls and serve immediately.*
Serves 4.

*To hold, place in freezer; remove 30 minutes before serving.

Per serving: Calories 127; protein 5 gm; carbohydrates 27 gm; fat <1 gm; cholesterol 0 mg; calcium 151 mg; sodium 41 mg. Exchanges: 1 1/2 fruit and 1/2 skim milk.

Banana Ice Cream Softie

2 cups banana slices (about 3 bananas)
1 tablespoon lemon juice
$1/4$ teaspoon banana or coconut extract, optional
$1/8$ cup honey
1 cup non-fat yogurt cheese

Arrange bananas on a baking sheet lined with waxed paper. Sprinkle with lemon juice to keep from discoloring. Place in the freezer for about 4 hours.

In a food processor (metal blade), process frozen bananas until powdery. Add the remaining ingredients and process until thick and smooth. Do not overprocess.

Spoon into 4 dessert bowls and serve immediately.*

Serves 4.

*To hold, place in freezer; remove 30 minutes before serving.

Per serving: Calories 178; protein 6 gm; carbohydrates 40 gm; fat <1 gm; cholesterol 0 mg; calcium 148 mg; sodium 42 mg. Exchanges: 2 fruit and 1/2 skim milk.

• NUTRITIONAL VALUES OF COMMON FOODS

Use this table to make informed dietary choices. All figures are approximate; actual values may vary depending on season, brand of product used, etc., and, with yogurt cheese, draining time and method. Abbreviations used are:

CHO = cholesterol
SOD = sodium
CAR = carbohydrates
CAL = calcium

PRO = protein
NA = information not available
tr = trace
<1 = less than 1

	CALORIES	FAT (gm)	CHO (mg)	SOD (mg)	CAR (gm)	CAL (mg)	PRO (gm)
Angel food cake, 1/16 cake	121	< 1	0	127	27	4	3
Apple, raw, 1 medium	81	<1	0	1	21	10	<1
Anchovy fillet, 1	8	<1	NA	147	0	9	1
Apricots, dried, 1/4 cup	78	<1	0	3	20	15	1
Avocado, 1 medium	324	31	0	21	15	22	4
Bagel, 1 (2 oz.)1							
egg bagel	150	1	5	360	29	NA	7
water bagel	150	1	0	320	30	NA	6
Baking powder, 1 tsp.	5	tr	0	312	1	239	tr
Banana, 1 medium	140	1	0	1	36	9	2
Beef bouillon							
regular, 1 cube	6	<1	0	864	1	NA	1
low-sodium granules,1 tsp.	11	<1	0	10	2	NA	<1
Beef, cooked, 4.5 oz.	241	8	115	76	0	16	40
Blueberries, raw, 1 cup	41	<1	0	4	10	4	<1
Blackberries, raw, 1 cup	37	<1	0	0	9	23	<1
Brandy, 1 Tbsp.	36	NA	NA	NA	NA	NA	NA

177

	CALORIES	FAT (gm)	CHO (mg)	SOD (mg)	CAR (gm)	CAL (mg)	PRO (gm)
Bread							
English muffin, 1	135	1	NA	364	26	92	4
hamburger bun	130	2	NA	240	22	NA	4
light	80	<1	0	190	21	NA	4
Italian bread, 1 slice	70	1	5	135	12	NA	NA
light, 1 slice	40	<1	0	80	8	NA	2
pita bread, 1/2 (1 oz.)	70	0	0	160	15	NA	3
pumpernickel, cocktail-size, 2	60	1	0	125	10	NA	2
rye, 1 slice	66	1	NA	174	12	20	2
cocktail-size, 2	50	1	0	135	9	NA	2
white, 1 slice	68	<1	<1	3	13	3	2
whole wheat, 1 slice	56	<1	<1	121	11	23	2
light, 1 slice	40	<1	0	80	8	NA	2
Broccoli, raw, 1/2 cup	12	<1	0	12	2	21	1
Broth, beef, 1 cup							
regular	19	<1	1	1358	2	5	1
low-sodium	11	<1	0	10	2	NA	<1
Broth, chicken, 1 cup							
regular, 1 cup	35	2	0	810	3	NA	1
low-sodium, 1 cup	30	2	1	76	2	21	2
Buttermilk, 8 oz.	99	2	9	257	12	285	8
Carrot, raw, 1 medium	31	<1	0	25	7	19	1
Cauliflower, raw, 1/2 cup	12	tr	0	7	2	14	1
Caviar, 1 oz.	84	5	96	704	1	88	9
Celery, 1/2 cup	9	tr	0	53	2	22	<1
Cheese, 1 oz.							
blue cheese	100	8	21	396	1	150	6
Cheddar							
regular	114	9	30	176	<1	204	7
reduced fat	80	5	20	210	1	NA	8
cream cheese, 1 oz.	99	9	31	84	1	23	2
Monterey Jack, regular	106	9	30	190	0	NA	6
reduced fat	80	6	20	160	0	NA	8

	CALORIES	FAT (gm)	CHO (mg)	SOD (mg)	CAR (gm)	CAL (mg)	PRO (gm)
Cheese, continued							
Parmesan, freshly grated	110	7	19	320	1	336	11
Swiss, regular	107	8	26	74	1	273	8
reduced fat, 1 Tbsp.	100	7	18	35	1	NA	8
yogurt cheese, 1 oz.							
from non-fat yogurt	20	<1	0	20	2	70	2
yogurt cheese, 1 cup							
from non-fat yogurt	160	0	0	160	17	560	18
from lemon yogurt (low-fat)	248	7	11	160	26	480	18
from plain low-fat yogurt	200	6	11	144	10	480	22
from vanilla yogurt (low-fat)	248	7	11	160	26	480	18
Chicken, cooked, 4.5 oz.							
white meat	220	6	108	98	0	19	39
dark meat	261	12	119	119	0	19	35
Chile peppers (can), 1/2 cup	17	<1	0	995	3	18	<1
Chili sauce, 1 Tbsp.	3	<1	0	191	1	1	<1
Chutney, 1 Tbsp.	41	0	0	26	8	5	<1
Corn chips, 1 oz.	154	10	0	202	15	35	2
Corn, creamed,							
low-sodium, 1/2 cup	93	<1	0	4	3	4	2
Cornstarch, 1 Tbsp.	63	tr	0	tr	7	0	tr
Crab meat, 1 oz.	26	<1	28	60	<1	12	5
Crackers							
Cheez-It (low-cholesterol), 12	70	4	<2	135	7	NA	1
Cheese Snack Sticks, 8	130	5	0	400	19	NA	4
graham cracker, 1 whole	54	1	NA	94	10	5	1
Kavli, thin crispbread, 2	24	tr	NA	32	8	NA	1
matzo, 1	119	<1	0	tr	25	0	3
melba rounds, 1 oz. , 10	120	<1	0	340	<1	NA	2
rice cake (plain), 1	35	0	NA	35	7	NA	1
rice cake, mini (plain), 6	50	0	NA	15	12	NA	1
Ritz, 1	18	1	0	32	2	5	<1
Ryvita (high fiber), 1	23	<1	0	10	4	NA	<1

	CALORIES	FAT (gm)	CHO (mg)	SOD (mg)	CAR (gm)	CAL (mg)	PRO (gm)
Crackers, continued							
Ry-Krisp, 1	25	<1	NA	48	5	2	1
saltines, 1	13	<1	NA	40	2	2	<1
Samurai Puffs, .7 oz.	90	3	0	60	15	NA	2
Wasa crisp bread (rye), 1	35	0	0	55	7	NA	1
water cracker, 1	14	<1	0	20	2	NA	<1
wheat, low-cholesterol, 8	70	4	0	170	9	NA	1
whole wheat, 1	16	<1	NA	22	3	1	<1
Zweiback toast, 1	30	1	NA	16	5	1	1
Cranberries, raw, 1/2 cup	23	tr	0	<1	6	3	<1
Cucumbers, 1/2 cup	7	tr	0	1	2	7	<1
Danish pastry, 1	179	10	NA	22	19	1	3
Dates, 1/4 cup	122	<1	0	1	33	14	1
Egg, 1 large	79	6	274	69	1	28	6
1 white	16	0	0	55	1	3	3
1 yolk	63	6	274	14	0	25	3
Eggplant, raw, 1/2 cup	11	tr	0	1	3	15	<1
Endive, Belgian, raw, 1/2 cup	4	tr	0	6	1	13	<1
Fish and seafood							
crabmeat, 1 oz.	26	<1	28	60	<1	12	5
imitation, 1 oz.	30	tr	5	275	3.5	NA	3.5
halibut, broiled w/butter, 3 oz.	144	6	42	114	0	15	21
lobster, 3 oz.	81	1	72	178	1	55	16
red snapper, 3 oz.	109	1	40	48	0	34	22
salmon, 3 oz.							
fresh, broiled with butter	155	6	40	99	0	NA	23
pink, canned (with bones)	120	6	30	329	0	167	17
pink, canned (no bones)	118	5	37	471	0	7	17
scallops, steamed, 3 oz.	96	1	46	227	0	99	19
shrimp, 3 oz.							
fresh	82	2	119	119	1	54	16
canned	99	1	127	119	1	97	21
sole, filet of, baked, 3 oz.	172	7	43	202	0	20	25

	CALORIES	FAT (gm)	CHO (mg)	SOD (mg)	CAR (gm)	CAL (mg)	PRO (gm)
French toast, frozen, 1 slice	85	2	NA	216	13	47	3
Green beans, cooked, 1/2 cup	22	<1	0	2	5	29	1
Horseradish, prepared, 1 Tbsp.	6	tr	0	14	1	9	<1
Ketchup, 1 Tbsp	16	<1	0	156	4	3	<1
Lemon juice, 1 oz.	8	0	0	<1	3	2	<1
Mandarin orange, 11 oz. can	116	<1	0	18	30	35	2
Margarine							
regular, 1 Tbsp.	101	11	0	152	0	4	0
light, 1 Tbsp.	49	6	0	138	tr	2	tr
Mayonnaise, 1 Tbsp.							
regular	99	11	7	78	<1	2	<1
cholesterol-free	50	5	0	80	1	NA	0
light	50	5	5	115	1	NA	0
Mushrooms, raw, 1/2 cup	9	<1	0	1	2	2	1
Mustard, 1 Tbsp.							
Dijon	15	1	0	195	1	19	1
yellow, low-sodium	10	<1	0	2	1	NA	1
Nuts, 2 Tbsp.							
almonds, dry roasted	101	9	0	2	4	49	3
macadamia	120	13	0	1	2	7	1
peanuts, unsalted	105	9	0	3	3	16	5
pecans	90	9	0	<1	2	5	1
pine nuts, 1 oz.	170	17	0	28	5	0	3
walnuts	96	9	0	1	3	14	2
Oil, 1 Tbsp.							
canola	120	14	0	NA	0	NA	0
corn	120	14	0	tr	0	0	0
olive	119	14	0	tr	0	0	0
peanut	119	14	0	tr	0	0	0
safflower	120	14	0	tr	0	0	0
Olives, black							
whole, 5	31	3	0	192	1	20	<1
chopped, 1 Tbsp.	11	1	0	69	<1	7	tr

	CALORIES	FAT (gm)	CHO (mg)	SOD (mg)	CAR (gm)	CAL (mg)	PRO (gm)
Olives, green, stuffed							
whole, 5	22	2	0	463	<1	12	<1
Onions, chopped, 1/2 cup							
green	13	tr	0	2	3	30	1
yellow	27	<1	0	2	6	20	1
Pancakes, plain, 1 small	61	2	20	152	7	58	2
Parsley, chopped, 1/2 cup	10	tr	0	12	2	39	1
Pasta, 1 oz. cooked	105	<1	0	1	22	4	3
Peanut butter, 1 Tbsp.	95	8	0	75	2	5	5
Peas							
green, cooked, 1/2 cup	67	<1	0	2	12	22	4
snow (Chinese peapods) 1 oz.	13	tr	0	1	2	13	1
sugar snap, 2.6 oz.	45	0	NA	5	9	NA	2
Peppers (bell), raw, 1/2 cup	12	<1	0	2	3	3	<1
Pear, raw, 1 medium	98	1	0	1	25	19	1
Pineapple							
fresh, 1/2 cup	38	<1	0	<1	10	5	<1
canned, in own juice, 1/2 cup	75	<1	0	2	20	17	<1
Pizza, cheese, 14-inch							
1/8 pizza	153	5	NA	456	18	144	8
Potato chips, 10	105	7	0	94	10	5	1
Potatoes, sweet							
baked, 1/2 cup	103	<1	0	10	24	28	2
Potatoes, white							
baked, 6 oz.	124	<1	0	9	29	11	3
boiled, 1/2 cup	68	<1	0	3	16	4	1
Pumpkin, canned, 1/2 cup	41	<1	0	6	10	32	1
Radishes, fresh, 1/4 cup	5	<1	0	7	1	6	<1
Raisins, 2 Tbsp.	62	tr	0	2	16	10	1
Salsa, bottled, 1 Tbsp.	5	<1	0	63	1	NA	<1
Seafood (see Fish and seafood)							
Spinach, frozen, 1/2 cup	27	tr	0	82	5	139	3

	CALORIES	FAT (gm)	CHO (mg)	SOD (mg)	CAR (gm)	CAL (mg)	PRO (gm)
Squash, cooked, 1/2 cup							
summer	13	<1	0	1	3	13	1
zucchini	14	<1	0	2	3	12	1
Strawberries, 1/2 cup	22	<1	0	1	5	10	<1
Sweetener, 1 Tbsp.							
honey	64	0	0	1	17	1	<1
maple syrup	48	0	0	2	12	20	0
molasses, light	46	0	0	7	13	58	0
preserves							
regular	54	tr	0	2	14	4	<1
artificial sweetener	6	<1	0	tr	1	1	<1
low-cal	24	0	0	23	6	1	0
sugar							
brown	52	0	0	4	13	12	0
white	48	0	0	<1	12	0	0
Tomatoes,							
fresh, 1 medium	24	<1	0	10	5	8	1
canned 1/2 cup	24	<1	0	195	5	32	1
juice, regular, 3/4 cup	32	<1	0	658	8	16	1
low-sodium	34	<1	0	6	8	13	1
paste, 1 Tbsp.	14	<1	0	11	3	6	1
Turkey, roasted without skin, 3 oz.							
dark meat	159	6	72	67	0	27	24
light meat	133	3	59	54	8	16	25
Turkey ham, 3 oz.	109	4	NA	848	<1	8	16
Waffles, 1 medium							
from recipe	141	9	22	164	11	51	3
frozen	95	3	NA	235	14	28	2
Wheat germ, 1 Tbsp.	27	1	NA	<1	5	3	2
Wine, 3 oz.	71	0	0	4	3	7	<1
Worcestershire sauce, 1 Tbsp.	12	0	0	147	3	15	<1

• *INDEX*

185

186

Crab
  appetizer, 64
  dip, hot, 38
  mold, Caribbean, 103
  salad sandwich spread, 79
Cranberry
  ice cream softie, 174
  -maple cheese, 129
Creamy bloody mary , 119
Creamy gazpacho, 118
Creamy taco soup, 123
Crescents, 153
Cucumber
  mold, 93
  soup, 115
  tea sandwiches, 69
Curry(ied)
  -cheese ball, 51
  eggplant soup, 117
  pea soup, 121
  shrimp spread, 43
  spread, easy, 43

D

Danish pastry, 154
  easy #1, 154
  easy #2, 154
Date(s)
  Honey-date spread, 136
  -nut spread, 136
Dijon dressing, 100
Dilly dip #1, 28
Dilly dip #2, 29
Dough, basic, 140
Dressing
  Calcutta, 96

caper, 95
Dijon, 100
green peppercorn, 98
mustard, 97
Neapolitan, 101
pecan parsley, 105
thousand island, 94

E

Eggplant soup, curried, 117
Eggs, information, 16

F

Fiesta puffs, 65
Fish spread, gefilte, 37
Frozen yogurt bars, 170
Fruit fondue, 133
Fruit ice cream softies, basic re-
  cipe, 170

G

Garlic-cheese spread, 47
Garlic-chive stuffed potatoes, 74
Gazpacho, creamy, 118
Gazpacho dip, 19
Gefilte fish spread, 37
Gingerbread, 155
Ginger lime dip, 130
Great granola bars, 164
Green peppercorn dressing, 98

H

Hawaiian cream, 135
Herb cheese, quick #1, 25

Orange spread, tangy Florida, 134

P

Pancakes, whole wheat, 145
Parsley cheese, 44
Pasta entree, 47
Pastry, Danish, 154
Peanut butter
  bran muffins, 156
  spread, easy lo-cal, 134
Pear ice cream softie, 175
Pea soup, curried, 121
Pecan parsley dressing, 105
Peppercorn dressing, green, 98
Pesto
  pasta sauce. , 49
  salad dressing., 49
  spread, 49
Pineapple ice cream softie, 171
Pita
  bread: pocket lasagne, 72
  chips, baked, 139
Pizza
  cheese, 73
  crust, 148
  vegetable, 85
Pocket lasagne, 72
Poppy seed cheese, Hungarian, 34
Potato-caviar bites, 56
Potatoes, stuffed
  broccol-cheese, 75
  garlic-chive, 74
  lemon-chive, 76

zucchini, 77
Potato salad, 99
  beef and, 100
  chicken and, 98
  sweet, 99
Pretzels, soft, 151
Puffs, fiesta, 65
Pumpkin bread, 146

Q

Quiche squares, 68
Quick
  breads (see Bread)
  herb cheese #1, 25
  herb cheese #2, 26

S

Sage-derby cheese, 22
Salmon
  mousso, 104
  salad sandwiches, 84
  stuffed tomatoes, 60
Salsa, 90
Sandwich buns, 165
Sauce, tomato, 91
Shrimp
  dip, 39
  mold, 102
  soup, 124
  spread, curried, 43
Snow peas, stuffed, 55
Sodium, information, 16
Soft pretzels, 151
Spice cake, applesauce, 163

Spinach
- -cheese bites, 57
- -cheese squares, 62
- dip, 20
- -onion spread, 33
Sticky buns, 162
Strawberry
- dip, 130
- ice cream softie, 172
Stuffed
- banana chiles, 66
- mushrooms, 54
- snow peas, 55
Sweeteners, information, 16
Sweet potato salad, 99

T

Taco
- dip, creamy, 123
- soup, creamy, 123
Tailgate treats, 80
Tangy Florida orange spread,
  134
Tempting tuna sandwiches, 83
Terrine, vegetable, 107
Tex-Mex cheesecake, 67
Thistle dip, 31
Thousand island dressing, 94
Tomato(es)
- salmon stuffed, 60
- sauce, 91
- soup, 119
Tortilla chips, baked, 138

Tuna
- pate, 41
- sandwiches, tempting, 83
- sandwich spread, basic, 82
Turkey
- burritos, 86
- salad, 105, 108
Twists, 148

V

Vanilla
- ice cream, 168
- topping, easy, 129
Vegetable
- cheese pie, 70
- dip, 24
- pizza, 85
- terrine, 106
Viennese liptauer, 35

W-Y-Z

Waffles, 166
Water chestnut dip, 42
Whole wheat muffins, 143
Whole wheat pancakes, 145
Yogurt bars, frozen, 170
Yogurt cheese
- recipe, 11
- information, 12-13
Yogurt Cheese Funnel, 13, 191
Zucchini stuffed potatoes, 77

• SHOPPING INFORMATION

•••*Snack to your Heart's Content! The Low-Fat, Low-Cholesterol, Low-Calorie Quick & Easy Cookbook.* 150 recipes. $9.95

•••*Not Just Cheesecake! The Low-Fat, Low-Cholesterol, Low-Calorie Great Dessert Cookbook.* 101 recipes. $9.95

•••*Really Creamy* ® Yogurt Cheese Funnel. The easy way to make yogurt cheese. Unmolds cleanly. $9.95

•••7-inch springform pan. Best size for cheesecake recipes in *Snack to your Heart's Content* and *Not Just Cheesecake.* Tin-plated steel, $6.95; or heavy-duty aluminum (steel clasp), $12.95

•••Exchanges calculated by the author, based on Weight Watchers ® program. Free.

•••Catalogue of Triad's books. Free.

These items may be ordered from Triad Publishing Co., 1110 N.W. 8th Avenue, Gainesville, FL 32601. Enclose payment plus shipping and handling: $2.50 first item, $1 each additional. Florida residents add 6% tax. (No charge for shipping free items.)

Subject to availability. All prices subject to change without notice.   (SHC 1/90)